# Complete Starter Guide to
# Bonsai

## Growing from Seed or Seedling—Wiring, Pruning, Care, and Display

David Squire

CRE▲TIVE
HOMEOWNER®

## About the Author

David Squire has a lifetime's experience with plants, both cultivated and native types. He studied botany and gardening at the Hertfordshire College of Horticulture and the Royal Horticultural Society's Garden at Wisley, Surrey. Throughout his gardening and journalistic careers, David has written more than 80 books on plants and gardening. He also has a wide interest in the uses of native plants, whether for eating and survival, or for their historical roles in medicine, folklore, and customs.

# CREATIVE
## HOMEOWNER®

Copyright © 2024 David Squire and Creative Homeowner

Creative Homeowner® is a registered trademark of New Design Originals Corporation.

Complete Starter Guide to Bonsai
Managing Editor: Gretchen Bacon
Acquisitions Editor: Lauren Younker
Editor: Joseph Borden
Designer: Wendy Reynolds

ISBN: 978-1-5801-1609-1

The Cataloging-in-Publication Data is on file with the Library of Congress.

We are always looking for talented authors. To submit an idea, please send a brief inquiry to acquisitions@foxchapelpublishing.com.

Printed in China
First Printing

Creative Homeowner®, *www.creativehomeowner.com*, is an imprint of New Design Originals Corporation and distributed in North America by Fox Chapel Publishing Company, Inc., 800-457-9112, 903 Square Street, Mount Joy, PA 17552.

# Contents

*Bonsai is an art everyone can master, creating a vast array of miniature trees and shrubs that will enrich your garden as well as indoors. Here is a spectacular example of an outdoor evergreen coniferous bonsai in the Bonsai Garden at Fairylake Botanical Garden in Shenzhen, China.*

# Introduction

Bonsai is both an art and a craft. It can be learned by novice gardeners and turned into a satisfying hobby, providing the opportunity to meet like-minded people through clubs and exhibitions.

Traditionally, bonsai was solely concerned with growing hardy outdoor trees, shrubs, and conifers, but more recently an innovation has been to grow tropical and sub-tropical plants indoors and to treat them in the same way as outdoor bonsai. Many outdoor bonsai enthusiasts have difficulty in accepting this innovation, but really it is just an extension of bonsai, enabling gardeners, perhaps without a garden, to enjoy growing dwarfed plants indoors. They are ideal for creating interest throughout the year.

Outdoor bonsai does not need a great amount of space, although the area must receive a good amount of sunlight and be protected from strong, blustery winds. Avoid positions where icy winds whip between buildings, as well as where eddies of turbulent wind are created by solid walls.

Bonsai does not have to be an expensive hobby, and although many enthusiasts start with an established bonsai bought from a specialist nursery, it is possible to raise your own plants from seeds and cuttings and to train them into a bonsai. It is also possible to convert a garden-center plant into a much-admired bonsai.

Bonsai is a highly stimulating and captivating hobby that will enthral both you and your family for many years.

## Seasons

Throughout this book, advice is given about the best times to look after plants. Because of global and even regional variations in climate and temperature, the four main seasons have been used, with each sub-divided into "early," "mid," and "late"—for example, early spring, mid-spring and late spring. These 12 divisions of the year can be converted into the appropriate calendar months in your local area, if you find this helps.

## Measurements

Both metric and imperial measurements are given in this book—for example 6' (1.8m).

# Gallery

← *Domoto Maple, Trident Maple (Acer buergerianum); formal upright style; original artist: Toichi Domoto; date of origin: ca 1850; in training as a bonsai since at least 1913; donated by Marilyn Domoto Webb to the Pacific Bonsai Museum. Believed to be the oldest bonsai in America, the 'Domoto Maple' was imported to the U.S. for exhibition in the 1915 Panama Pacific Exposition in San Francisco, California.* PHOTO BY WINIFRED WESTERGARD FOR PACIFIC BONSAI MUSEUM.

↓ *Frankenpine, Japanese Black Pine (Pinus thunbergii) with nails and metal; In training since 2015; informal windswept style Bonsai and container by Aarin Packard.* PHOTO BY WINIFRED WESTERGARD FOR PACIFIC BONSAI MUSEUM.

↑ Creeping Juniper raft (Juniperus horizontalis); group windswept style; date of origin: 1950; original artist: John Naka; in training as a bonsai since 1957. PHOTO BY WINIFRED WESTERGARD FOR PACIFIC BONSAI MUSEUM.

← California Juniper (Juniperus californica); semi-cascading driftwood style; date of origin unknown. Original artist: Harry Hirao; Donated to Pacific Bonsai Museum by Mel Ikeda. PHOTO BY WINIFRED WESTERGARD FOR PACIFIC BONSAI MUSEUM.

← *Japanese Maple forest (Acer palmatum); original artist: Warren Hill; in training as a bonsai since 1970.* PHOTO BY WINIFRED WESTERGARD FOR PACIFIC BONSAI MUSEUM.

↓ *Visitor at Pacific Bonsai Museum, 2022.* PHOTO BY WINIFRED WESTERGARD FOR PACIFIC BONSAI MUSEUM.

↑ *Festive Eastern White Pine (Pinus strobus) bonsai, informal upright style. Adorned with holiday decorations, this bonsai presents a unique blend of traditional art and seasonal cheer.* PHOTO BY DENIS RODINGER.

← *Lush Brazilian Rain Tree (Chloroleucon tortum) bonsai, bushy upright style. Thriving in its container, this bonsai showcases the species' characteristic delicate foliage and robust trunk.* PHOTO BY DENIS RODINGER.

→ *Burt Davy's Fig (Ficus burtt-davyi), admired for its striking aerial roots and dense canopy of green, lends a miniature forest feel to any collection. Informal semi-cascading style.* PHOTO BY MARK FIELDS.

← *This display features a variety of species, including a mature deciduous bonsai taking center stage, flanked by smaller trees with lush green canopies. This arrangement exemplifies the art of bonsai, where each tree complements the others to create a balanced and peaceful miniature landscape.* PHOTO BY DENIS RODINGER.

← *Maidenhair Tree (Ginkgo biloba), renowned for its fan-shaped leaves and revered for its ancient lineage, stands as a living fossil in bonsai form. Bushy style.* PHOTO BY MARK FIELDS.

→ *Japanese White Pine (Pinus parviflora), celebrated for its soft blue-green needles and gracefully sculpted trunk, stands as a testament to the artful practice of bonsai. Informal upright style.* PHOTO BY MARK FIELDS.

# Getting Started

# What Is Bonsai?

## ■ Is bonsai a difficult hobby?

Bonsai is relatively simple to do, but it requires dedication throughout the year. Plants need to be watered and fed, while other activities include pruning, wiring, and pinching. None of these is arduous, and the skills needed can be learned and honed over a year or so. However, growing bonsai is a hobby that continues to reveal new facets, and the precise skills needed when looking after one plant may need to be modified for another.

## Bonsai Definition

The definition of bonsai is growing a tree—or several trees in a group—in a shallow container. By pruning branches, leaves, and shoots, as well as roots, these plants are encouraged to remain miniature and to resemble trees growing in the wild. Incidentally, the word bonsai is both singular and plural, and therefore can be applied to a single plant or to a group.

There are both outdoor bonsai and indoor bonsai, and in temperate climates this means growing winter-hardy trees, shrubs, and conifers outdoors throughout the year. In such climates, indoor bonsai (tropical and sub-tropical plants) are left indoors throughout the entire year.

## The Miniature Tree

*Miniature specimens of bonsai are ideal where space is limited. Although small, they reveal all the fascinating qualities of larger and more dominant bonsai.*

## Indoor Bonsai (Chinese)

Sometimes known as Chinese bonsai, and created from tropical and sub-tropical plants, this is a relatively recent innovation in the art of growing bonsai. These are tender plants that, in temperate climates, need to be grown indoors throughout the year. However, in warm climates, they can also be grown outdoors.

The range of plants suitable for growing as indoor bonsai is more limited than for the outdoor types, and includes *Bougainvillea*, Crassulas, *Ficus benjamina* (Weeping Fig), *Gardenia, Nandina domestica* (Chinese Sacred Bamboo), *Olea europaea* (Olive), *Schefflera arboricola*, and *Syzygium malaccense* (Malay Apple).

*Indoor bonsai creates dramatic features throughout the year. Here is a dignified indoor bonsai displayed on a low, decorative table that harmonizes with the symmetry of the plant.*

Outdoor bonsai can be displayed either individually or in groups, creating attractive features throughout the year.

## Outdoor Bonsai (Japanese)

Sometimes known as Japanese bonsai, and created from winter-hardy trees, shrubs, and conifers, outdoor bonsai is the long-established form of this art. Within this book, all outdoor bonsai are assumed to be growing in a temperate climate. Temperatures in warmer climates may not enable some of these plants to be grown. The range of outdoor bonsai subjects is wide and encompasses deciduous trees, shrubs, and both evergreen and deciduous conifers.

Deciduous trees and shrubs include Acers, *Aesculus hippocastanum* (Horse Chestnut), *Betula pendula* (Birch), *Buxus sempervirens* (Box), *Cercidiphyllum japonicum* (Katsura Tree), *Fagus sylvatica* (Beech), *Morus nigra* (Black Mulberry), *Salix babylonica* (Willow), and many others.

Deciduous and evergreen conifers used in bonsai include *Cedrus libani* (Cedar of Lebanon), *Chamaecyparis, Ginkgo biloba* (Maidenhair Tree), Larches, *Metasequoia glyptostroboides* (Dawn Redwood), and *Taxus baccata*.

Flowering trees and shrubs encompass Forsythia, Flowering Cherries, Jasmine, and Wisteria; fruiting types include Pyracanthas and *Malus*.

This columnar outdoor bonsai (Chamaecyparis obtusa) forms a distinctive and dignified outline and is ideal for positioning where lateral space is limited.

# Spirit and Esthetics

### ■ Is there an ideal bonsai shape?

There are many different styles of bonsai (see pages 16–17); some have an upright and formal shape, others lean, and a few reveal a cascading nature. They all have their own ideal proportions, and should exhibit balance and harmony within themselves as well as between the plant and the container. Each bonsai must create the impression of being a miniature form of a full-sized tree—an inspiration from nature as well as a replication.

## Spirit and Soul

The spirit and soul of outdoor bonsai can be traced back a thousand or more years to China, and is claimed to have associations with religious thoughts about naturalism and mountains, trees, and rocks having a soul. Some bonsai historians suggest that the gnarled and contorted shapes of bonsai represent the bodies of people in the next world and without mortality. Other authorities claim that a form of growing miniature trees was known much earlier in India. Whatever the origination of bonsai, its spirit and soul were absorbed into Japanese culture in the eighth century, where it was perfected into an art steeped in beauty and correctness. It is this correctness of purpose, and desire for perfection in mirroring nature, that encapsulates the soul of bonsai.

Nowadays, the spirit of bonsai is also continued through indoor bonsai where, in temperate climates, tropical and sub-tropical plants are grown indoors throughout the year (see pages 67–77 for more details).

*The simplicity of bonsai is encapsulated in the nobility revealed by this aged representation of a juniper, an evergreen conifer with needle-like leaves. Plain and uncluttered backgrounds help to highlight plants.*

### Introduction to the West

Before the beginning of the 20th century, bonsai was little known outside Japan. In 1909, an exhibition of bonsai was held in London, where it caused a sensation. The art of bonsai was taken up by many people and is now popular throughout the world.

↗ *In earlier times, bonsai were claimed to be representations of people in the next world.*

→ *Groups of trees growing naturally on a hillside reflect the ideal of simplicity in bonsai.*

# Esthetics

Bonsai must be pleasing to the eye, creating through style, shape, and size an impression of a tree nurtured solely by nature and its environment. It may have an upright, leaning, windswept, or cascading nature, replicating trees in the wild.

## Design Factors

There are three main design factors; the arrangement of branches, the trunk, and the roots. When old and exposed, roots are a distinctive feature (see below right).

## Size and Scale

Bonsai range in size from 4' (1.2m) down to 6" (15cm), or even less. Large trees are easier to look after than miniature ones, especially as the amount of water given is less critical; small amounts of composts are more at risk from excessive watering.

## Viewpoint

Most bonsai have a "face" or "front" side, which reveals the plant at its best. Keep this in mind when creating an attractive yet natural shape through pruning and wiring. Curves and the general shape can be seen best from the plant's side, rather than from the ends of the container.

| WHAT MAKES A BONSAI LOOK GOOD? | |
|---|---|
| **FEATURE** | **GENERAL GUIDANCE** |
| Apex | Should give an impression of being natural, not manipulated into an unnatural shape. |
| Trunk | Elegant and tapering. |
| Inter-branch | Creates a sense of space, as well as allowing light and air **space** to circulate between and around the branches. |
| Branches | Lowest branch should be the largest and most dominant, and about one-third of the way up the trunk. |
| Roots | Surface roots and lower trunk give the tree a mature nature. |
| Shape | For upright formal and informal styles, this should be somewhat triangular (see pages 16–17 for a range of styles). |
| Position | In an oval or rectangular pot, the tree should be positioned **of tree** centrally along the width, and about one-third of the distance from one of the ends. |
| Tree and | These must be in proportion to each other and an approximate **container in** guide (for upright styles) is that the container's length should **proportion** be two-thirds to three-quarters of the tree's height. |
| Color | The container should complement the tree, in color and **harmony with** proportion. Shades of dark blue, brown or green harmonize **container** with most trees. |
| Compost | Surface must look natural. |
| Container's | Approximately the same as the diameter of the trunk near to **depth** its base. However, cascading bonsai have deeper containers. |

## Exposed Roots

Old, exposed roots are a further attraction and create the impression of maturity. They also give the bonsai greater stability and can extend in all directions from the trunk. They are able to continue the flowing line of many attractive trunks.

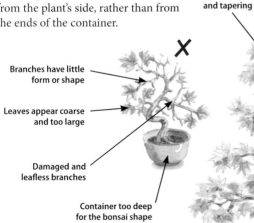

**✗**

Branches have little form or shape

Leaves appear coarse and too large

Damaged and leafless branches

Container too deep for the bonsai shape

*↗ → The tree must be in "balance" with itself as well as with its container. A too-large pot would dominate the tree and immediately capture attention. Its color and shape must also complement the tree.*

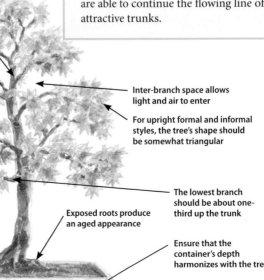

Trunk elegant and tapering

**✓**

Inter-branch space allows light and air to enter

For upright formal and informal styles, the tree's shape should be somewhat triangular

The lowest branch should be about one-third up the trunk

Exposed roots produce an aged appearance

Ensure that the container's depth harmonizes with the tree

# Styles of Bonsai

## ■ Are there many different styles?

Bonsai styles range from upright and in small groups to cascading. These styles mimic shapes revealed by trees in nature, perhaps blown by wind and leaning, cascading over a cliff, or in small clusters. Here is a picture parade and detailed explanations of the main styles revealed by bonsai. Some can be displayed on flat surfaces, while others need to have areas in which their branches can freely cascade, perhaps from a special stand.

## Range of Styles

The most important identification of style is the angle at which the trunk grows in the container. The formal upright tree is, by nature, upright and with branches that create an approximately triangular outline, whereas an informal upright has a slightly leaning trunk which imparts a more relaxed nature.

Relaxed and informal styles are becoming more popular than formal types and this probably mirrors the increasingly relaxed nature of society.

### Outdoor/Indoor?

**Outdoor bonsai** has a more aged history than **indoor bonsai**, which is a recent innovation. Aficionados of outdoor bonsai often look with disdain on indoor bonsai, but it is only another facet of the same great art of bonsai. For indoor bonsai, see pages 67–77.

### Formal and upright

*Triangular outline, but not symmetrical. Subjects suited to this style include needle-bearing conifers such as Larches, Pines, Junipers and Spruces, but not informal trees nor those with a fruiting nature.*

### Informal and upright

*Fundamentally, an irregular triangular outline, with a bent trunk (usually at its base) and leaning no more than 15 degrees. Both evergreen conifers and deciduous trees create this relaxed style.*

### Semi-cascading and cascading

↗ → *These have a relaxed and informal nature. Semi-cascading (above) has, in part, a horizontal habit and gives an impression of growing out from the top of a cliff or stretching over water. The cascading type (right) evokes the image of a wild tree growing on and over a steep cliff.*

### Leaning

↖ *Sometimes known as a slanting style, the trunk leans throughout most of its length, at about 45 degrees, and gives the impression of a tree growing in a windswept area. Occasionally, the trunk is curved.*

## Twin and multi-trunks

This adds further interest and form a more dominant feature than a single-stemmed plant. They can be formed of evergreen conifers or deciduous trees chosen for their foliage.

## Windswept

This style has an even more windswept nature than the leaning (slanting) type, with stems trained to appear especially windswept. Evergreen conifers are particularly suited to this style which, when displayed, must not be constricted by other bonsai.

## On a rock

Formed of single trees, as well as groups of plants. There are two main styles: the root-over type involves roots spreading down and over a rock (shown), while the other is where a tree is planted on the rock.

## Groups and landscape

*➜ ⭨ These mimic woodland, forests, and groves and, if formed by deciduous trees, look especially attractive in spring when new leaves are forming. In autumn, many trees assume rich autumnal colors. Avoid symmetry—it is better to have a few taller plants towards one side than to create an even-topped display.*

*The lower display is a raft type, where some stems are initially horizontal and introduce greater interest at compost height.*

### Style Representations

Bonsai styles represented here are depicted through evergreen conifers. However, many of these styles are also suitable for deciduous trees, including flowering and fruiting types.

## FLOWERING BONSAI

Few bonsai features capture as much attention as a flowering tree. To many people, cherry trees are the epitome of spring, while *Malus* (Crab Apples), Lilac, Forsythia and Azaleas are other superb subjects for outdoor bonsai.

They are winter-hardy plants but when in flower need a wind-sheltered position, especially those that create their display in spring. Sudden gusts of wind, as well as heavy rainstorms, quickly destroy these displays.

Birds can also be a problem as they are soon attracted to developing buds. If plants are at risk, a bird-proof covering or cage is the only answer until buds cease to be attractive, although young leaves are tempting.

# Tools and Materials

## ■ What are the basic tools?

The range of bonsai tools is extensive, but initially it is possible to look after your plants with just a few of them. Indeed, basic toolsets are available and contain essential equipment. Always buy good-quality tools, as they will then last a lifetime. If possible, hold cutting and wiring tools in your hand before buying them to ensure that they feel comfortable and easy to use. This is especially important for women, who usually have small and less muscular hands.

## Specialist Tools

Apart from the tools and materials featured on these pages, unusual equipment includes "bending jacks" and "bending levers." They are used to bend branches, and look like candidates for a medieval torture chamber. So infrequently are they needed that, for most bonsai enthusiasts, they need little attention.

A gardening knife is useful, especially for severing roots that have become adhered to the inside of a container. Thin-bladed but resilient knives are especially helpful.

Large, old table forks—with their prongs levered apart—can be used as rakes, but those with prongs too close together tend to draw away and remove too much compost.

## Brushes

A light, soft-bristled paintbrush is useful for dusting debris from plants and tidying up the soil's surface. Additionally, an old but still straight-bristled toothbrush helps in the cleaning of trunks and branches (see page 19).

## Spoons

An old, large, redundant tablespoon will come in useful for moving and positioning compost while potting and repotting plants. Spoons are inexpensive but invaluable.

## Scissors

### Keep them sharp and not strained

These have many uses, from general cutting to trimming shoots and leaves. Never use a pair of scissors for cutting material too thick for them—the blades will bend, become twisted, and never again be able to make clean cuts. Strained scissors bruise leaves, stems and shoots, often causing parts to die.

## Wiring tools

### For cutting and twisting wires

Wire-cutters are used to cut wires employed to train branches and trunks, as well as to secure rootballs in containers when being initially potted or repotted. Pliers are used to twist and secure the wires that hold the rootball in place.

↗ *Wires are needed both for general purposes and for training and shaping branches and trunks.*

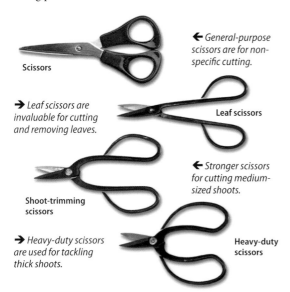

**Scissors**

← *General-purpose scissors are for non-specific cutting.*

→ *Leaf scissors are invaluable for cutting and removing leaves.*

**Leaf scissors**

← *Stronger scissors for cutting medium-sized shoots.*

**Shoot-trimming scissors**

→ *Heavy-duty scissors are used for tackling thick shoots.*

**Heavy-duty scissors**

→ *General wire snips are ideal for cutting wire.*

→ *Heavy-duty snips are invaluable for cutting thick wire.*

→ *Pliers are essential for manipulating wire.*

→ *Long-nosed pliers enable detailed manipulation of wire.*

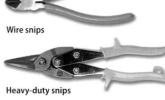

**Wire snips**

**Heavy-duty snips**

**Pliers**

**Long-nosed pliers**

## Pruning and Cutting Tools

### Matching their size to the bonsai

The size and nature of pruning tools need to be matched to the size and type of bonsai. Large trees need large, strong tools, whereas small ones require fine and delicate ones. Never use small cutting tools on thick branches. Small cutting tools, often with long handles and tapering cutting blades, are essential when working on miniature trees.

Concave branch-cutters

Spherical knob-cutters

↗ *Concave branch-cutters are used for general-purpose branch-cutting.*

↑ *Spherical knob-cutters are ideal for tidying up old wounds and the stubs of branches.*

Folding pruning saw

→ *Secateurs are useful for pruning tough branches.*

Secateurs

↗ *Small, folding saws cut without squeezing branches.*

→ *Woodworking gouges are tools for general-purpose cutting and manipulating.*

→ *Wound sealant is essential for helping cuts to heal quickly.*

Wound sealant

Woodworking gouges

### Turntable

This is a refinement that enables a tree to be worked upon without the need to move around it. It is an ideal piece of equipment for gardeners who are not mobile and have to sit in one position, perhaps in a wheelchair.

## Potting Tools and Equipment

### Essential for when potting and repotting

These are essential when first potting a tree to create a bonsai feature, as well as later when established plants need repotting, perhaps every 2–3 years. The tools encompass compost firmers (chopsticks or skewers), soil scoops, root hooks and potting trowels. Other potting materials are pieces of plastic mesh, wire to secure the plant, and potting compost. Composts suited to specific plants are detailed on page 22.

Chopsticks

↗ *Chopsticks are ideal for manipulating and firming compost around roots.*

Plastic mesh

↗ *Plastic mesh is essential for preventing compost falling out of drainage holes in containers.*

Soil scoop

↗ *Soil scoops enable compost to be added to containers when potting and repotting.*

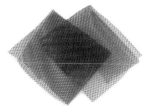

## TOOL CARE

After each use, wash and thoroughly wipe dry all equipment. Tools are best stored in a toolbox and put in a damp-proof shed. If they are allowed to become dirty and caked with grime, they will not work properly and may even encourage the introduction and spread of diseases.

Some tools can be bought in sets and in tailor-made cases. In this instance, keeping the tools in good condition is made easy.

↙ *Root hooks are used to draw old compost from soil balls when repotting.*

Root hooks

Brush

↗ *A soft brush is invaluable for smartening plants and compost.*

Potting trowel

↖ *Potting trowels help in moving compost when potting and repotting plants.*

# Containers for Bonsai

## ■ What container should I have?

The range of bonsai containers is wide and their prime purpose is to accommodate the plant and its compost. They also create a firm base for the plant. Additionally, they must complement the plant, in size, shape, and color. It is essential that the container does not dominate the plant. Most containers are relatively shallow, but those for cascading and semi-cascading plants are taller and better suited to stems that trail.

## Container Essentials

Apart from holding sufficient compost (so that the plant grows strongly for 2–3 years between each repotting) the container must be frost-proof and with enough drainage holes to enable any excess water to escape. Additionally, by threading string or wire through the holes the rootball is held in place while it is becoming established in the compost.

Fruiting bonsai types need more compost than foliage types. This is because the compost will be required to hold a greater reservoir of water, in order to aid in the swelling of the fruits.

The interior of a container is not glazed, but the outside can be either glazed or unglazed. Consider how the color of the pot and the type of decoration can enhance the bonsai.

*Wisterias create a feast of color, with drooping clusters of fragrant flowers. The color and scallop-edged detailing of this circular container enlivens the scene.*

*The stern-looking, tapering square shape and dark, earthy color of this elegant container are perfect for a cascading Juniper. The emphasis is on balance and strength.*

## HOW THE CONTAINER CAN COMPLEMENT THE BONSAI

### The Bonsai

The position of the plant in a pot is important. For example, in an oval or rectangular pot, the subject is best positioned towards one end, perhaps one-third of the length. However, position it centrally on the width of the container. Take care not to constrict roots too close to the side of a container, as the plant will then become insecure.

### The Container

The size, shape and color of the container must harmonize with the tree. Before selecting a pot, have a look at other plants and containers that create harmonious combinations.

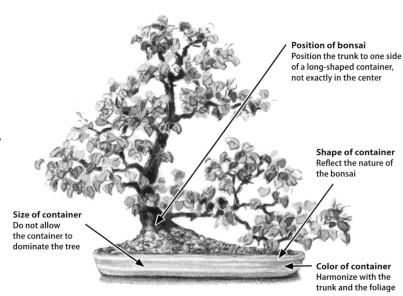

**Position of bonsai**
Position the trunk to one side of a long-shaped container, not exactly in the center

**Shape of container**
Reflect the nature of the bonsai

**Size of container**
Do not allow the container to dominate the tree

**Color of container**
Harmonize with the trunk and the foliage

# A Guide to Container Options
## Begin by choosing an appropriate shape of pot

| DRUM | RECTANGULAR | OVAL | CASCADE |
|---|---|---|---|

| **Ideal for heavy and rugged bonsai, such as evergreen conifers.** | **Suitable for many bonsai styles; select depth to suit plants.** | **Choose for individual and group bonsai; select depth to suit plants.** | **Essential for cascading displays; they raise the base of the plant off the ground.** |

**Small, terracotta, drum shape**

*Unglazed and with a masculine nature; also ideal for bamboo bonsai.*

**Medium-depth, pale gray, rectangular shape**

*This pale color is ideal for a group of deciduous bonsai, such as Maples.*

**Shallow, off-white, oval shape**

*This pale container is ideal for a group of deciduous trees.*

**Tall, ochre, square, for cascading bonsai**

*A tall square container, ideal for simple bonsai with just a few trailing stems.*

**Medium-sized, dull-green, drum shape**

*A glazed pot suitable for an upright bonsai, especially literati.*

**Deep, ochre, rectangular shape**

*A neutral color, suited to large, heavy-looking bonsai.*

**Medium-depth, mauve, oval shape**

*This strongly colored container may suit some flowering bonsai.*

**Medium-height, blue, hexagonal, for cascading bonsai**

*A decorative hexagonal container; avoid using for large, dominant bonsai.*

**Large, deep, terracotta, drum shape**

*Deep and unglazed, with a nature ideal for evergreen conifers.*

**Shallow, terracotta, rectangular shape**

*Ideal for group plantings.*

**Medium-depth, terracotta, oval shape**

*This unglazed container with a "natural" color is suitable for evergreen conifers.*

**Low, green, square, for cascading bonsai**

*Heavy and square with ornate feet, for bonsai with large, long, trailing stems.*

**Deep, pale gray, oval shape**

*This deep container is ideal for thick-trunked bonsai.*

## Getting the color right

Colors used for bonsai containers must be restrained. Usually they are restricted to shades of dark blue, brown, green or off-white.

**Flowering trees** are sometimes put in colorful containers but usually it is better to use more subdued and subtle colors.

**Ceramic glazes** when subtle and discreet suit some form of bonsai, especially flowering trees—but they must not dominate the plant.

**Container's size:** The tree and pot must be in proportion to each other, otherwise a large pot will dominate a small tree. An approximate guide is that a container's length should be two-thirds to three-quarters of the tree's height.

# Composts and Potting

## ▮ What is the purpose of compost?

The function of compost is to retain moisture for a plant's growth, yet be sufficiently well drained to prevent waterlogging. It is essential that compost contains air to enable roots to breathe and beneficial soil organisms to be active. Additionally, compost must contain plant foods that are easily and readily available to a plant's roots. The weight and amount of compost in a container also helps to create a secure base for a plant.

## Range of Composts

Different bonsai need specific potting composts and, in general, there are three mixtures that are used. They are formed of various combinations of clean, friable, pest- and disease-free loam, sphagnum moss peat and granite grit. Details of these mixtures and their particular uses are given in the quick guide to composts on the right.

In earlier years, some bonsai enthusiasts used mixtures of good garden soil, well-rotted leafmold and coarse, clean sand or grit. This often contained pests and diseases that soon caused damage to roots and the leafy parts of plants. Additionally, although this may have been tolerable for traditional outdoor bonsai, with the introduction of indoor bonsai few people want creepy-crawlies wandering about their living rooms and over their furniture.

## Mixing Composts

When mixing your own compost, it is essential that the area is free from contamination. Choose a flat, clean surface.

All ingredients should be dry when mixed and passed through a sieve to give a particle size of up to ⅜" (5mm). Too many fine particles tend to clog up the compost, preventing the entry of air and the drainage of excess moisture, eventually causing the plant's death.

## Initial feeding

When initially potting or repotting a plant, the compost should not contain fertilizers, as they will rapidly burn and damage young and developing roots. However, once a plant is growing strongly in spring, feeding can begin (see pages 36–37 for details). Weak feeds are better than strong ones.

### Proprietary compost mixtures

Proprietary compost mixtures are available and these are best bought in amounts that can be used within a few months. Reseal the bag and store them in a cool, dry, pest-free shed.

| A QUICK GUIDE TO COMPOSTS | |
|---|---|
| **PURPOSE** | **MIXTURE** |
| **Mixture One**<br>Basic soil mixturethat suits most bonsai | • One part loam<br>• Two parts sphagnum moss peat<br>• Two parts granite grit |
| **Mixture Two**<br>Especially free-draining mixture that suits many woodland trees | • One part loam<br>• One part sphagnum moss peat<br>• Three parts granite grit |
| **Mixture Three**<br>Essential for plants that dislike lime in the soil | • One part loam<br>• Three parts sphagnum moss peat<br>• One part granite grit |

*Note: The various parts of these composts are mixed by bulk, not by weight. Always use a clean container to measure them.*

### POTTING: WHAT TO AIM FOR

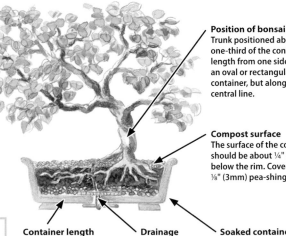

**Position of bonsai**
Trunk positioned about one-third of the container's length from one side of an oval or rectangular container, but along a central line.

**Compost surface**
The surface of the compost should be about ¼" (6mm) below the rim. Cover with ⅛" (3mm) pea-shingle.

**Container length**
The container's length should be between two-thirds and three-quarters of the tree's height.

**Drainage**
Piece of plastic-coated mesh placed over the drainage hole.

**Soaked container**
Clean container which has been thoroughly soaked in water, if earlier unused.

# How to Prepare a Pot

Before potting, always thoroughly prepare the container so that the drainage hole (or holes) is covered with plastic-covered mesh that will both prevent compost falling out and ensure that excess moisture can escape. Additionally, there must be a method of securing the rootball in position. The method shown here is for a container with two holes in the base.

Where there is only one hole in the container's base, pass a wire through the hole, around a headless nail and back into the pot (an example of this is shown on pages 28–29, when root-pruning and repotting).

**1** Select a container that harmonizes with the tree, and soak it in clean water for several days. Then remove and allow to dry before use. Very dry containers absorb water from the compost and may deprive the plant of moisture.

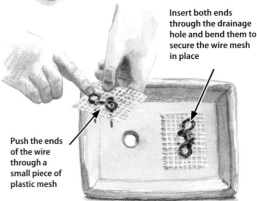

Insert both ends through the drainage hole and bend them to secure the wire mesh in place

**2** Use plastic-coated wire to secure a piece of plastic-covered mesh to the inside of the drainage hole (sometimes two) in the container's base. At each end of a piece of wire, form a small loop with a short tail. These will later be used to hold the mesh in position.

Bend the wire to form two separate loops

Push the ends of the wire through a small piece of plastic mesh

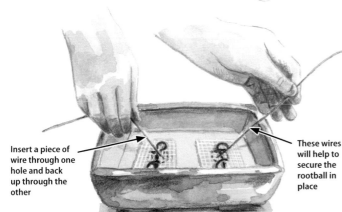

Insert a piece of wire through one hole and back up through the other

These wires will help to secure the rootball in place

**3** Place a piece of mesh inside the container and over the hole. Then put the wire on the other side and push the two 'tails' through the hole and mesh. Bend both ends of the wire to secure the mesh firmly in position.

**4** To secure the rootball in position—until new roots are sufficiently developed to hold the tree firmly—insert a long piece of plastic-coated wire through one hole in the base of the container and back up through the other one. Ensure that the wire is long enough to be tied over the rootball. (In earlier times, garden string was an alternative.)

## INITIAL STAGES

Sometimes seedling trees can be gathered from the wild, but permission is needed before digging them up, and even then success is not assured. Plants can be raised from seeds, which is an inexpensive but lengthy method, as germination is not rapid and styling the plant is a long-term task. Raising plants through cuttings is faster and the nature of the progeny more assured than by seed propagation. However, some species, such as Pines, are difficult to raise through cuttings and are therefore best grown from seeds.

For successful home-raised plants—which have been regularly repotted—there comes a time when they can be put into a bonsai container. The technique is much the same as for repotting (see pages 28–29), but do not tease away so many roots—just those that are extra thick and long. The plant, after a couple of years in its new container, can then be repotted and more radical root-pruning can be attempted.

### Repotting

Repotting an existing tree after 2–3 years in the same container is detailed on pages 28–29. This also applies if you started your bonsai collection with an established plant in a container.

# Seasonal Care (Outdoor Bonsai)

## ■ Is there a routine of care?

Routine care varies from one season to another, and while spring is usually an active period, care is also needed throughout the other seasons. Watering and feeding are routine activities, closely dictated by the seasons and the growth of plants. Wiring and pruning are other seasonal activities that are fully described and illustrated in this book. The early pages in this book are especially devoted to giving practical advice.

## Seasonal Displays

Throughout the year, bonsai creates magnificent displays, including flowering trees in spring, broad-leaved deciduous trees in summer (together with further flowering plants), brilliant autumnal colors from deciduous bonsai, and stately evergreen conifers in winter. The range of outdoor bonsai is wide—see pages 43–66.

In addition to caring for bonsai throughout the year, it is essential to display them properly (see page 27), so that they can be admired—as well as worked upon easily. This is especially important for gardeners who cannot bend down easily or are in wheelchairs. It involves having display benching at an accessible and workable height.

### SPRING

↙ *This evergreen shrub* Camellia japonica *is around 50 years old and about 2½' (75cm) high. In late winter and spring, it creates a wealth of beautiful flowers.*

→ *The evergreen Azalea* Rhododendron kiusianum *creates a stunning display in the spring. This magnificent bonsai is at least 80 years old and about 2' (60cm) high and wide.*

This is often the busiest season in the bonsai calendar. All plants are becoming active, although the precise time will depend on the plant and local weather patterns (see below). Growth is beginning on deciduous trees and young buds are starting to break into growth. There are many routine tasks to undertake, including the following.

- Repot and root-prune (in spring or early summer), when buds start to swell (see pages 28–29).
- Pinch back shoots on some bonsai (see pages 32–33).
- Wire deciduous trees, just before their buds start to unfold (see pages 34–35).
- Wire conifers while they are dormant, from early winter to early spring (see pages 34–35).
- Check whether the compost needs watering (see pages 36–37). The compost should not become dry.
- Feed bonsai (see pages 36–37).
- From early spring to late summer, spray plants with insecticides and fungicides (see pages 40–41).

← *The deciduous* Crataegus cuneata, *an Ornamental Thorn, reveals a wealth of flowers in late spring and early summer. This 30-year-old bonsai is 18" (45cm) high and 14" (35cm) wide.*

## Variations in Climate

Even within a distance of 100 miles (160km) further south or north, the climate can vary. Some places are sheltered from cold winds, with hills that create warm havens for plants, while windswept areas feel the wrath of sub-zero winds. Therefore, throughout this book, suggestions such as "when buds start to break" are given rather than a calendar of seasonal dictate.

## SUMMER

Flowering bonsai—as well as deciduous trees such as Acers, with their intricately shaped and beautifully colored leaves—create magnificent displays. Deciduous conifers, such as *Larix decidua, Metasequoia glyptostroboides* and *Taxodium distichum*, will be revealing their new leaves, which look especially attractive when caught by the sun's rays. There are many routine tasks, including the following.

- Repot and root-prune (in spring or early summer), when buds start to swell (see pages 28–29).
- Check if the compost needs watering (see pages 36–37).
- Feed bonsai (see pages 36–37).
- From early spring to late summer, spray plants with insecticides and fungicides (see pages 40–41).

## AUTUMN

This is the season of autumnal color, although with the onset of global warming in some areas this occurs later than in previous years. Some of the Acers are especially attractive when their leaves assume rich colors, from yellow through to red. Evergreen conifers continue their stateliness and dignity and help to maintain interest. There are still several routine tasks to undertake.

- Wire deciduous trees, before they become dormant (see pages 34–35).
- Check if the compost needs watering (see pages 36–37).
- Feed bonsai (see pages 36–37).

*Many deciduous trees assume rich colors in autumn. They can be displayed on their own or in groups with conifers.*

*Many deciduous trees reveal stunningly attractive leaves, especially when young and during early summer. This group creates a beautiful feature throughout summer. Some trees also have leaves that assume rich coloring in autumn.*

## WINTER

Early and mid-winter are quiet times in the bonsai year, but toward late winter in some areas, growth can be seen, and this gives encouragement that plants are waiting to create their displays. Conifers continue to provide shape and color interest throughout even the dullest weather. Even the bare trunks and branches of deciduous trees are attractive when low winter light glances off them. Winter, by its nature, is a dull period, but plants still need regular attention.

- Wire conifers while they are dormant, from early winter to early spring (see pages 34–35).
- Check that birds are not damaging plants.
- Use a soft brush to dust off snow from branches before it freezes and causes damage.

# Indoor Bonsai

These are tropical and sub-tropical plants which are kept indoors in temperate climates and therefore need different conditions and treatment to outdoor bonsai, which are winter-hardy, outdoor plants. For detailed information about looking after indoor bonsai, see pages 68–69. Additionally, pages 67–77 feature many indoor bonsai plants.

# Buying Bonsai

### ■ How do I start a bonsai collection?

There are several sources of established bonsai—such as specialist nurseries and garden centers—as well as inexpensive ways to start a collection, from sowing seeds to taking cuttings and air-layering branches. Young plants can be dug up (with permission) from the wild and potted. Additionally, there is the possibility of buying a shrub or tree from a garden center or nursery and, through radical pruning, converting it into an attractive bonsai.

## Starting with Bonsai

### Specialist Nurseries
This is usually a safe way to buy an established bonsai, especially if the nursery is reputable and has been established for many years.

### Garden Centers
Usually, bonsai are well established, but beware of buying a plant newly potted and pruned to create an instant bonsai.

### Raising Your own
Propagation by means of seeds, cuttings, or air-layering is explained on pages 38–39. Part of the fun of bonsai is raising your own plants.

### Modifying Plants
Established plants can be bought from garden centers or nurseries and converted, through radical pruning, into bonsai (see page 30).

### CHOOSING A HEALTHY BONSAI

For assured success, buy your bonsai from a reputable, long-established bonsai nursery, where you can get expert advice about buying and looking after your plants. Never start with an unhealthy plant.

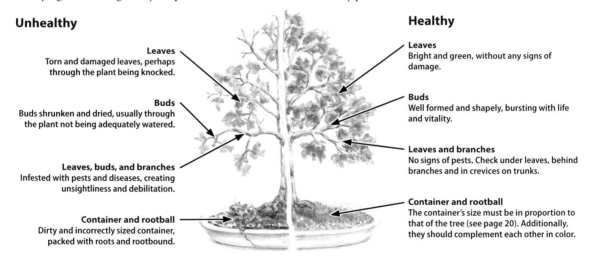

**Unhealthy**

**Leaves**
Torn and damaged leaves, perhaps through the plant being knocked.

**Buds**
Buds shrunken and dried, usually through the plant not being adequately watered.

**Leaves, buds, and branches**
Infested with pests and diseases, creating unsightliness and debilitation.

**Container and rootball**
Dirty and incorrectly sized container, packed with roots and rootbound.

**Healthy**

**Leaves**
Bright and green, without any signs of damage.

**Buds**
Well formed and shapely, bursting with life and vitality.

**Leaves and branches**
No signs of pests. Check under leaves, behind branches and in crevices on trunks.

**Container and rootball**
The container's size must be in proportion to that of the tree (see page 20). Additionally, they should complement each other in color.

↗ *When buying a bonsai, thoroughly check it over—don't be reluctant to ask questions about the plant and container.*

## Getting Your Bonsai Home

An established bonsai is expensive and therefore needs care when taking it home. When using a car:

- Don't take young children with you, as often they cannot resist poking at plants;
- Don't take a dog with you;
- Don't drive fast over pot-holes and speed-ramps;
- Don't leave the bonsai in strong sunlight;
- Don't position it in a draught from an open window.

### Let the Buyer Beware!
Buying a plant from a garden center and converting it into a bonsai is an excellent way for a home gardener to create a bonsai. However, it can be an expensive way of buying an "established" plant if nurseries do the same and sell it under the pretense that it is an authentic bonsai. If in doubt, ask for assurance that it is an established bonsai.

# Exhibiting Bonsai

## ◼ I've got my bonsai—so what's next?

Like many hobbies, once bonsai has captured your enthusiasm and confidence has been gained in growing them there is a desire to show them to other aficionados of the art. There is much to be gained from "rubbing shoulders" with experts and gaining an insight into improving plants and displaying them for exhibition. Local gardening clubs often welcome a bonsai display, even in general and non-specialized exhibitions of plants.

## Displaying Bonsai at Home

Outdoor bonsai are able to live outside throughout the year. They need a position sheltered from strong, blustery wind, as well as in good light. They can be displayed in several ways, on supports formed of timber that has been treated with a wood preservative or on concrete constructions.

- On staging, perhaps attached to a garden wall if it forms an attractive background. Unfortunately, such positions are often shaded for much of the day.
- On free-standing staging, positioned out of shadows and at various heights.
- On "monkey poles," at various heights and basically a vertical support with a platform at the top.

## Checking the Trunk and Branches

All parts of a bonsai must look perfect when exhibited. Below are ways to smarten trunks and branches, and bring plants to perfection.

- Use tweezers to pull off dead bark from the trunk, but take care not to scar it. Remove a little at a time.
- An old, dry toothbrush is ideal for removing dust, as well as splashes of dried water and compost from trunks and branches.
- Clean off algae by slightly moistening an old toothbrush. Take care not to rub too hard. Initially, use a soft brush.
- Clean around the base of the trunk, where small pieces of rubbish may accumulate. Small tweezers are often useful.

## MAKING FINAL PREPARATIONS FOR EXHIBITION

After the trunk and branches are clean, check the compost and container. Pick off dead leaves and conifer needles which may have fallen on the compost. There may also be odd pieces of prunings. Should two exhibits have comparable qualities, judges will check the bonsai's presentation, and therefore it is well worth paying extra attention to the compost and container.

**1** When the surface is free from debris, add further compost. Do not mound up the compost unnecessarily—leave a gap at the edges between the compost's surface and the top of the container's rim.

**2** To enhance the compost and to create a natural-looking surface, add a thin layer of moss; press it into the surface and, at the same time, dampen it with clean water.

## Watering Bonsai

Before taking a bonsai for exhibition, water the compost several times to ensure that it is thoroughly moist. Flowering bonsai that wilt could have their display irreparably damaged, while deciduous trees in full leaf soon wilt when the compost is dry.

**3** The final task is to wipe dust off the sides and rim of the container. Then, use a piece of cloth lightly coated with vegetable oil to wipe the container's sides to give it extra "eye appeal."

# Root-Pruning and Repotting

## ■ When should I repot?

After a plant's initial potting, a bonsai tree will grow in the same pot and compost for several years without any disturbance. Thereafter, it needs repotting every two or three years, in spring or early summer when buds are starting to swell. If repotting is neglected, the compost becomes packed with roots and the plant's growth is retarded; the foliage loses its attractiveness and eventually the plant has to be discarded if the plant is not given fresh compost.

## Step-by-Step Sequence

Repotting is not difficult and if taken step-by-step is easily accomplished. A clean, dry pot is essential. Do not try to reuse the existing pot; thoroughly clean it before further use.

If the tree is young and growing strongly, select a pot fractionally larger than the existing one. However, if the plant is well established, use a clean pot of the same size until the roots are potbound. At that time, use a slightly larger pot.

Always select a pot that complements the plant, in size, shape and color. It should not dominate the plant and be a focus of interest. It is the plant that is important.

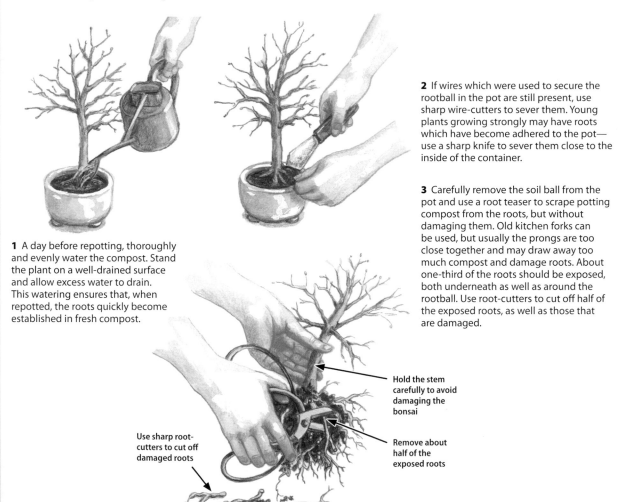

**1** A day before repotting, thoroughly and evenly water the compost. Stand the plant on a well-drained surface and allow excess water to drain. This watering ensures that, when repotted, the roots quickly become established in fresh compost.

**2** If wires which were used to secure the rootball in the pot are still present, use sharp wire-cutters to sever them. Young plants growing strongly may have roots which have become adhered to the pot—use a sharp knife to sever them close to the inside of the container.

**3** Carefully remove the soil ball from the pot and use a root teaser to scrape potting compost from the roots, but without damaging them. Old kitchen forks can be used, but usually the prongs are too close together and may draw away too much compost and damage roots. About one-third of the roots should be exposed, both underneath as well as around the rootball. Use root-cutters to cut off half of the exposed roots, as well as those that are damaged.

Hold the stem carefully to avoid damaging the bonsai

Use sharp root-cutters to cut off damaged roots

Remove about half of the exposed roots

**4** Select a fresh pot and soak it in water for several days. Allow it to dry before use. Cut small pieces of plastic-coated wire mesh and place over the inside of each hole. Hold them in place with pieces of plastic-covered wire.

**5** To secure the plant, pass a piece of garden string or plastic-coated wire through the hole, around a headless nail, and back into the pot. Later, the ends are tied over the rootball. Sever the wire or string as soon as roots fill the pot.

**6** Sprinkle a mixture of perlag or clean flint chippings over the wire mesh. An alternative is well-washed ¼" (6mm) pea-shingle. This ensures good drainage. Then, add a thin layer of potting compost (for suitable mixtures, see pages 22–23).

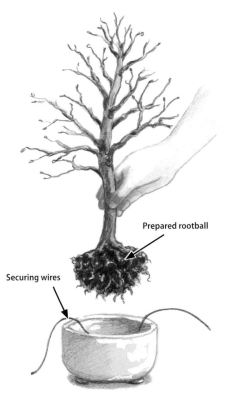

Prepared rootball

Securing wires

**8** When the roots are correctly positioned, pull up the ends of the string or wire and tie them over the rootball.

**9** Use a compost firmer (resembles a chopstick) to firm potting compost over and around the roots and to remove air pockets.

**7** Place the rootball in the pot and adjust the thickness of compost in the pot's base so that its top is slightly below the rim—about ¼" (6mm) should do it. If, when repotting is complete, the compost is too high, it is difficult to thoroughly water the compost.

**10** Sprinkle a thin layer of ⅛" (3mm) pea-shingle over the surface; it keeps the compost moist, as well as cool in summer.

**11** Water the compost by standing the pot in a shallow bowl of water. When moisture seeps to the surface, remove and allow any excess to drain.

# Pruning

## ◼ Does my bonsai need regular pruning?

There are three main reasons for pruning bonsai. The first is fundamentally to change the shape of a non-bonsai tree into a bonsai form. The second is, over several years, to change a young seed- or cutting-raised plant into an attractive bonsai. Additionally, there is the possibility of buying an "established bonsai" from a reputable nursery, when only maintenance pruning is needed. Nevertheless, regular pruning is essential to create an attractive plant.

## Types of Pruning

Bonsai experts tell of two main ways to create a bonsai by pruning. These are:

- **The subtraction method** (sometimes known as pruning to shape) is when an established tree, perhaps 3–4 years old, is bought in a pot from a garden center and unnecessary shoots and branches are then cut away to create a bonsai. It is a quick way to create a bonsai—perhaps taking only minutes. After being pruned, the tree is usually left for a year or two, when less radical pruning is needed to maintain its shape.

- **The addition method** is when a bonsai is started from a seed- or cutting-raised plant (see pages 38–39) and gradually, through pruning, acquires the desired shape. Clearly, this takes several years.

Leaves and stems become congested and unsightly

The foliage and branches assume an attractive shape

***Without pruning.*** *When pruning is neglected, plants soon lose their attractive shape and become a jungle of shoots.*

***With pruning.*** *Regular pruning enables light and air to circulate around and between the branches and leaves.*

### PRUNING A DECIDUOUS TREE

Maintenance pruning a deciduous tree is best performed in winter, when it is free from leaves and all of the branches and twigs can be clearly seen.

Some bonsai experts suggest that when pruning Acers (Japanese Maples) shoots are best cut back to ½" (12mm) above a bud. Later, after it has died back, the shoot can be tidied up. It is claimed that this prevents damage to buds.

Where thick branches are cut, use a wound sealant.

### Making the Job Easier

- Concave branch-cutters enable a cut to be made close to the trunk.
- Spherical knob-cutters, with their strong cutting action, are ideal for cutting off branch stubs.

**1** Use sharp scissors to cut out twigs or branches that cross each other and create congestion. Use branch-cutters on stems too thick to be cut by scissors. Use clean, accurate cuts.

**2** Cut out twigs and branches that are growing towards the tree's center and decreasing the circulation of air. Ensure that cuts are cleanly made and do not tear or rasp shoots.

**3** Where large and unsightly ends of branches remain after cutting out congested twigs and branches, use a strong pair of branch-cutters to cut them out cleanly.

## PRUNING A CONIFER

Maintenance pruning an evergreen conifer involves cutting out congested and crossing branches and twigs to allow light and air to enter the plant. However, unlike when pruning deciduous trees, long stubs can be left to create a *jin*. This has no English translation but means a stub that enhances the bonsai. To make the stub appear natural, use pliers to remove bark and slightly crush it. Do not leave torn or dead shoots on the surface of the compost.

### Design factors with conifers

- Simplicity of outline creates the greatest visual impact. Congested conifers confuse the eye.
- Keep the conifer's height in proportion to the length of the container (see pages 20–21).

**1** Use sharp scissors to cut out secondary branches that are growing upwards and, later, would spoil a branch's neat and well-defined outline. Aim to remove all congestion.

**2** Use branch-cutters to remove small branches. However, remember to leave some foliage at the end of each branch, both to continue growth and to draw sap to its end.

**3** To create a bushy nature, along and at the ends of branches, use fingers to pinch off the tips of shoots. Pinching out is not quick, but well worth undertaking (see pages 32–33).

## TWO UNUSUAL STYLES

**The broom style** is gaining increasing interest and at its best is like a domed and inverted twiggy broom, evenly covered with twiggy shoots. It is not suited to evergreen trees, rather to twiggy deciduous species such as *Zelkova serrata* (Japanese Elm) and some Maples. It is a difficult style to create and, for experience, it is useful to start with a bought tree for pruning and conversion into a broom style.

- Initially, use branch-cutters to remove low, somewhat twiggy branches growing from the trunk.
- Cut out crossing branches so that several equally spaced main branches are formed.
- Cut off large and heavy branches that are much larger than the other branches that will form the "head."
- Cut off the ends of shoots to leave a dome of equally spaced branches.
- In later years, regularly cut back shoots until a broom-like head has been created.

**The literati style** appears to defy all rules about bonsai, but is increasingly popular. It has a tall nature, with a fairly thin trunk and just a few branches at its top. The style suits most evergreen conifers and deciduous trees with a rugged nature, such as *Crataegus* (Hawthorn). It is possible to start with a plant from a garden center.

- Use branch-cutters to cut off low branches, so that the main ones will be at the top of the trunk.
- At the top, completely cut out coarse and heavy branches, leaving about five main branches (this must be formed of an odd number).
- Use wire to shape the remaining branches so that they have an irregular and slightly downward nature, a facet of this design.
- Use scissors to create a balanced head of foliage.

# Sealing Cuts

Cuts on bonsai are best covered with a wound sealant to aid rapid healing and to prevent the entry of diseases. It is easily applied by squeezing a tube of it. Do not use excessive amounts, as once a cut is covered with a sealant any extra will just be wasteful.

Incidentally, using sharp cutting tools, which have not been distorted through cutting too-large branches, encourages rapid healing.

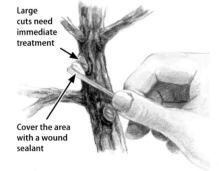

Large cuts need immediate treatment

Cover the area with a wound sealant

*Never risk the possibility of infection entering cut stems—treat cut surfaces immediately they are made during pruning.*

# Pinching

## ◼ What is pinching?

Also known as "pinching out" or "pinching back," pinching is a way to train or shape a tree by using your fingertips to pull off tender, new shoots. It can be used on deciduous trees, conifers including Juniper, Cryptomeria, Pine, Spruce, and Fir, and flowering and fruit trees. It is essential to break off the shoot cleanly, without causing damage to other shoots or foliage. The techniques and timing of pinching varies, and these are explained and illustrated on these pages.

## Pinching Techniques

Pinching out shoots initiates the development of fresh, young growth and is a form of maintenance pruning. Plants become bushier and with an attractive covering of young shoots and leaves. On some plants, without utilizing this technique vigorous shoots at their top grow faster than lateral ones and create a top-heavy and imbalanced appearance.

### DECIDUOUS TREES

Beginning in early spring, pinch back young shoots throughout the growing season: the tree must be growing strongly. Regular and frequent pinching gives better results than only occasionally pinching back a few shoots. In general, allow five new leaves to develop on a young branch, then pinch back to the first one or two at the top of the tree, and the first three or four young leaves on other parts of the tree. Always pinch back to a bud that points in the direction you want a branch to grow (see right).

If shoots have leaves that grow in pairs—with a bud in each leaf-joint and from the opposite side of a stem—one of each pair should be pinched back to create an asymmetrical appearance (see below, left).

With some species of Maple and *Zelkova*, all of the foliage can be nipped off in early summer, so that the tree is bare of leaves. This induces a fresh array of leaves that are daintier in size and more decorative. Never pursue this method with needle-leaved evergreens.

### Pinching a deciduous shoot

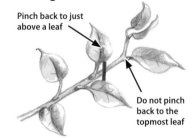

Pinch back to just above a leaf

Do not pinch back to the topmost leaf

*Regularly pinch back shoots throughout the growing season, rather than just occasionally.*

### Leaves which grow in pairs

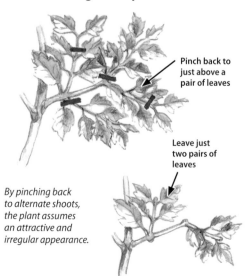

Pinch back to just above a pair of leaves

Leave just two pairs of leaves

*By pinching back to alternate shoots, the plant assumes an attractive and irregular appearance.*

### Encouraging a fresh crop of leaves

All of the foliage removed in early summer

Fresh crop of young, attractive leaves

*To encourage a fresh array of young and exceptionally dainty and small leaves, nip off all of the leaves in early summer. However, remember that doing this will mean that the bonsai is not so attractive early in the year.*

## FLOWERING TREES AND FRUIT TREES

The timing for pinching these bonsai is different from that used for deciduous trees, and must be timed so as to leave the developing flower buds intact. For example, Azaleas are pinched just after their flowers fade. Of the five new shoots that appear, usually only two are retained, and these are pinched back to leave two or three leaves. Later, during the same growing season, Azaleas are again pinched back, but less severely.

## EVERGREEN CONIFERS (JUNIPER AND CRYPTOMERIA)

These conifers produce new shoots throughout their growing season, when a few soft tips can be pinched out almost daily. However, during this period it is essential that the tree is producing young, healthy growth.

For the scale-leaved Junipers, gradually remove tips of shoots.

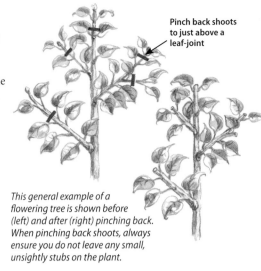

Pinch back shoots to just above a leaf-joint

*This general example of a flowering tree is shown before (left) and after (right) pinching back. When pinching back shoots, always ensure you do not leave any small, unsightly stubs on the plant.*

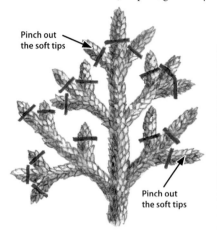

Pinch out the soft tips

Pinch out the soft tips

### Needle-Leaved Conifers

When pinching bonsai with needle-like leaves, take care not to nip through the leaves that remain on the plant. If left, they will turn brown and may cause decay. Leaves damaged in this way are also unsightly.

✓ Cleanly pinch out the entire tip

Do not cut through the tip and leave part of it ✗

## PINES, SPRUCES, AND FIRS

These are evergreen conifers, which each year produce their main growth in spring. Therefore, you should pinch out young shoots during that period, removing half or more of each one just as individual needles appear.

Cleanly pinch off young shoots

*It is essential to pinch off the shoots while they are still young and relatively soft.*

## Disbudding Pines

If the needles of a pine become too long in relation to the size of the bonsai, about every third spring, pinch off or use sharp scissors to remove all buds. This will dramatically change the bonsai's appearance, but the new buds and needles that develop during the following season will be smaller and have a more delicate appearance.

This disbudding technique is frequently used to keep pines looking both compact and attractive.

Pinch off the buds

*Create a more delicate and attractive bonsai Pine by pinching off buds every three or so years.*

# Wiring

## ■ What is wiring?

Wiring is a way of changing the shape of a branch or trunk. Copper wire (of various thicknesses) is wrapped around a branch or trunk at an angle of about 45 degrees, and left in place for up to a year. It is performed on both deciduous and evergreen trees, and once installed needs to be regularly checked to ensure that it is modifying the tree's shape but not cutting into the bark. The time to wire a bonsai is suggested below.

## How and When?

Using wire to shape a bonsai is, in theory, possible throughout the year, but is best performed on deciduous trees slightly before the buds start to unfold in spring or, alternatively, before they become dormant in autumn. Evergreen trees can be wired at any time, while conifers should be wired when dormant, from early winter to early spring.

Wires are wrapped around trunks in an anticlockwise direction, and the thickness of the wire should be just sufficient to hold the trunk or branch in place. Once the wires are in position, the trunk or branch can be carefully bent into the desired position. Do not keep bending the limb backward and forward, as this will cause damage. If the desired shape does not please you, unwind the wire and leave the tree alone for six months or so.

↗ *If a wire cuts into the bark, then either it has been there too long or it has been applied too tightly.*

→ *Wire is being used here to create a gentle, pleasing curve in the growth direction of the bonsai's main trunk.*

## Getting the Technique Right

The angle at which the wire is wound influences its ability to hold the branch or trunk in the correct position. For tapering and thin stems, the wires can be spaced further apart.

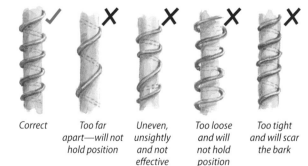

| Correct | Too far apart—will not hold position | Uneven, unsightly and not effective | Too loose and will not hold position | Too tight and will scar the bark |

### Removing the Wire

This needs to be done with great care, as there is a risk of damaging the tree. Unfix the wire at its upper end and carefully unwind. Usually, it is best to remove it in small pieces. Where the bark has been damaged, use a wound sealant.

### Wiring Essentials

Length of time the wire is left in place ~ this depends on the tree.

- Young growth is easier to manipulate and retains its position more quickly than old wood.
- Leave wire in place on deciduous trees for 3–6 months.
- For evergreens, a period of 6–12 months is needed to change the shapes of branches and trunks.

**Type of wire** ~ Traditionally, annealed copper wire has been used. However, plain or anodized aluminium wire is gaining increasing acceptance. Nevertheless, copper wire is still the choice of many bonsai enthusiasts, especially as it is less obtrusive than aluminium and is best for conifers.

**Thickness of wire** ~ The thickness of the wire depends on the size of the branch or trunk. As a guide, choose a gauge (thickness) of wire that is one-sixth to one-third of the diameter of the branch or trunk.

## SHAPING A TREE

Correctly wiring a tree needs experience, and therefore it is wise initially to try this technique on a few spare branches of a non-bonsai tree. It is essential that the wire is evenly wound around a branch or trunk. Before wiring a tree, check that a pair of wire-cutters and pliers (for twisting the wire) are to hand.

Cut a length of wire—slightly more than one-third longer than the length of the area to be wired—of the correct thickness (see opposite page).

### Double-Wiring

Occasionally, double-wiring is needed to remodel a tree. The first stage is to apply a single wire, at a 45-degree angle. Then secure a further wire into the compost and wind it around the trunk in exactly the same manner.

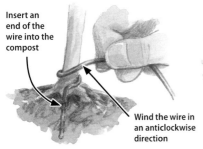

Insert an end of the wire into the compost

Wind the wire in an anticlockwise direction

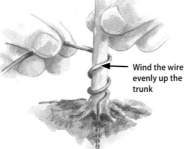

Wind the wire evenly up the trunk

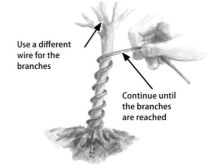

Use a different wire for the branches

Continue until the branches are reached

**1** Insert one end of the wire into compost behind the trunk. This will hold the end secure and prevent the wire coming loose. Then, in an anticlockwise direction and initially almost horizontally with the compost, bend the wire around the trunk.

**2** Continue to wind the wire around the trunk, ensuring that the distance between the coils is even, in an anticlockwise direction and at a 45-degree angle. The diagram on the opposite page shows the correct technique, as well as incorrect ones.

**3** Continue to wire the rest of the trunk. Do not deviate from it by starting with the same wire on a branch; branches, invariably, are narrower and can be given a thinner wire. It is then possible to manipulate trunk and branches separately.

## SHAPING A BRANCH

Thinner wire is usually needed for branches than that used for trunks. Start wiring branches from the lowest one, not the topmost. Cut a length of wire—slightly more than one-third longer than the length of the area to be wired—of the correct thickness (see opposite page). Ensure that wire-cutters and pliers are to hand.

Branches are usually wired separately, but where a couple are nearly opposite the same piece of wire can be used.

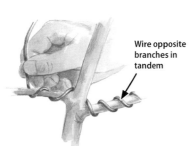

Wire opposite branches in tandem

Secure the end of the wire

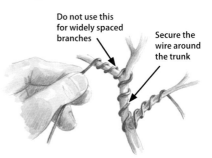

Do not use this for widely spaced branches

Secure the wire around the trunk

**1** If a branch is being wired in conjunction with another one, perhaps opposite, ensure that the wire is first looped over, not under, the branch. If it goes under, the branch may snap when bent.

**2** Where a branch cannot be wired as a continuation of another one, first bend the wire around the trunk and back along the branch. This secures the wire, which can then be wound around it.

**3** Where two branches, perhaps nearly opposite, are wired at the same time, wind the wire (at an angle of 45 degrees) around the trunk to ensure it is secure. Then wind it around the branch.

# Watering and Feeding

## ■ How should I water my bonsai?

Throughout their entire lives, bonsai require great care with watering. Like all plants, they need water, although in larger and more frequent amounts during summer, as they are growing strongly in this season. In winter, when resting and dormant, they will not require as much. Watering plants in containers is more difficult than those in beds in a garden. This is because, unless the compost is well drained and can readily escape from a container, there is a risk of the compost remaining too wet.

## More or Less?

Knowing when to water a plant is a skill that needs careful judgement, but it is one that can be learned. Because bonsai are usually grown in shallow containers which, relative to the size of the plant, do not hold much compost, it is essential to water plants daily during spring, summer, and into autumn. During winter, outdoor bonsai usually gain sufficient moisture from rain and, perhaps, snow. You should, however, regularly check bonsai which are in an unheated greenhouse or cold frame. Keep the compost moist, but not saturated.

Indoor bonsai will need watering throughout the year, but less in winter. In centrally heated rooms, regular watering is essential in order to prevent the compost becoming dry. Plants near radiators will need more attention than those positioned towards the room's center.

### WATERING OUTDOOR BONSAI

Water bonsai in the evening, after the sun has gone down. This ensures that the compost remains moist all night and into the morning. However, through hot summers, also water during the day if compost shows signs of becoming dry, but take care not to splash moisture on the foliage. The sun's rays may cause water droplets to act as a lens, intensifying its power and burning the leaves.

### Watering-can

Use a long-necked watering-can to reach plants without touching other bonsai. Both metal and plastic types are available.

### Use Clean Water

Only use clean water, and keep the inside of the watering-can clean. If dirt gets into the can, it can block the fine holes in the spray head. If the spray head is blocked, pull it off and wash it in water; also, blow through the holes and shake it.

### Watering Dos and Don'ts for Outdoor Bonsai

**Do:**
- Water in the evening, after sunset.
- Water during spring, summer and autumn.
- Keep the compost moist; if neglected, the foliage and buds shrivel.

**Don't:**
- Splash leaves with water while in strong light.
- Water during winter, unless plants are in an unheated greenhouse or cold frame.
- Water the foliage of deciduous trees, and especially plants when in flower or bearing fruits.

### Watering the soil and roots

Use a watering-can with a fine rose (turned upward) to water the compost. This prevents compost in newly potted or repotted containers being washed about. Gentle but thorough watering is essential—do not just dampen the surface.

### Dampening the foliage

Dampen the foliage of outdoor plants only during summer and when in a shaded position. This is best restricted to conifers with needle-like leaves; do not spray the foliage of deciduous trees and especially those bearing flowers or fruits.

Gently spray with clean water

Do not disturb the compost

# Feeding

Like all other plants, bonsai need to be fed regularly, although after they are repotted (see pages 28–29), you should always wait until the plant is displaying active growth before applying fertilizers.

If feeding is neglected, plants will not grow healthily and appear attractive. From spring to autumn, apply a balanced general fertilizer.

## FEEDING, WATERING, AND MISTING INDOOR BONSAI

Indoor bonsai are becoming increasingly popular. In earlier times, outdoor bonsai were often taken into a cool room for a few days at a time in order to create an indoor display, but this often upset the plant's seasonal nature.

Unlike outdoor bonsai, watering is needed throughout the year, although less in winter; but much depends on the plant and the temperature of the room.

Position an indoor bonsai where it creates a major feature in a room. However, it should not be in direct sunlight, in a draught, or where it can be readily knocked by animals or children.

## Applying fertilizers

Fertilizers are applied in two basic forms: liquid and solid. The latter encompasses powder, granules, and pellets. Liquid fertilizers are diluted in water, applied at watering times, and are soon available to roots. Unfortunately, heavy and persistent rain often leaches them from the compost. Powdered fertilizers are added to water. Granular plant foods are sprinkled on the compost's surface and are available to plants over a longer period.

The fertilizer requirements of plants vary throughout the year. From spring to autumn a general fertilizer is needed, but in autumn one low in nitrogen but high in potassium (potash) and phosphorus (phosphate) is better. Proprietary fertilizer mixtures are available; always adhere to the instructions on the packet. Do not be tempted to use fertilizer too strongly.

## Soaking the rootball

Standing the container, with the tree, in a bowl shallowly filled with water is an ideal way to water a newly potted tree, or one where the compost has become too dry to readily absorb moisture. When moisture percolates to the surface, remove the plant and allow any excess water to drain away.

## Feeding and watering

Use a small jug or watering-can to water and liquid-feed plants. Take care not to splash the foliage.

Never use fertilizers too strongly—a weak solution is better

Water the surface evenly

## Misting indoor bonsai

Many indoor bonsai are native to the tropics and therefore welcome having their leaves cooled by a misting with clean water.

Use a fine mist

Always use clean water to mist plants

## WATERING AND FEEDING: TROUBLESHOOTING

| SYMPTOM | LIKELY CAUSE | CORRECTING THE PROBLEM |
|---|---|---|
| Lack of growth, especially in spring | Lack of food and water | Water the compost thoroughly and then add a fertilizer |
| Leaves become yellow, especially on lime-hating plants such as Azaleas, *Enkianthus* and Stewartias | Wrong fertilizer or compost | Use an ericaceous fertilizer; also, check that the compost used did not contain lime |
| Leaves wilt | Usually insufficient moisture, but can also be too much water | If the compost appears dry, stand the container in a bowl shallowly filled with water until moisture seeps to the surface. If the compost is wet, use tissue to soak up and remove moisture and do not add further water until moderately dry |

# Raising New Plants

## ◼ Can I raise my own bonsai?

The usual way to increase plants is by seeds or cuttings, but experienced bonsai growers also graft and air-layer plants. Here, we show how to sow seeds and take cuttings, as well as the technique of air-layering. The seed-coats of some trees and shrubs need to be softened before sowing; this is known as stratification and is explained on the opposite page. Remember that it may take several years before a well-formed bonsai is created.

## Air-Layering Shrubs and Trees

Many shrubs and trees with low-growing branches can be layered at ground level. An adaptation of this technique is air-layering, enabling branches that cannot be lowered to ground level to be layered. The Chinese developed this technique many centuries ago, and more recently in the tropics and sub-tropics, it was known as gootee-layering and marcottage. A reservoir or water in a pot, together with a wick, were used to keep the compost moist in the warm climate. Rooting usually took place within six months.

In temperate climates, the technique used to prepare a stem on an outdoor tree is to make two cuts, about the width of the stem apart, on a healthy stem, and to remove the bark between them. Do this just before growth begins in spring. Around the cut, secure a 3" (7.5cm) high plastic pot, cut partly in half so that the drainage hole encircles the stem. Use insulating tape to secure it in place. Then, fill with equal parts moist peat and sharp sand, firming it around the cut stem. Keep the compost moist. When roots form, sever the stem below them, remove the plastic pot and transfer to another pot.

*Another form of air-layering involves covering a cut stem with moist sphagnum moss and encapsulating it in plastic.*

*A young bonsai seedling tree.*

### Buying Plants Versus Raising Your Own

It is always possible to visit a bonsai nursery and to buy a well-established plant that has consumed much skill and dedication in its development, but it is even more exciting to have raised a few plants yourself and to be able, with great pride, to show them to friends. Whether the plants you grow are from seeds or cuttings, raising and training takes several years. During this period, however, it is certain that your knowledge and experience of bonsai will be greater than if you remained with plants bought from a bonsai nursery.

*A young acacia.*

### Seeds or Cuttings?

Germinating and raising plants from seeds is less expensive and needs fewer pieces of equipment than when taking cuttings. Additionally, Pines are usually raised from seeds because their high resin content deters cut stems healing and producing a callus, which is vital before roots can form. Incidentally, grafting is possible with Pines.

However, raising plants from cuttings is a more visually exciting way of increasing plants than sowing seeds.

### Where to Buy Seeds

Seeds for bonsai are available direct from seed companies as well as many specialist sellers of bonsai equipment. Seed "kits" are available, but are often expensive. It is also possible to collect your own seeds, but there is always the risk of them not producing the desired plants.

## SOWING SEEDS

Many bonsai can be inexpensively raised from seeds. Collections of bonsai seeds, mainly deciduous trees and shrubs, but including a few evergreens, are on sale from specialist seed suppliers. They are available in mixtures of up to 40 different species and varieties, and provide an ideal way to raise your own plants. Seeds of trees and shrubs need to be stratified (see right) before being sown, and then sown thinly so that the seeds are spaced out and subsequent seedlings can be moved without disturbing seeds yet to germinate.

Fill a seed pan with well-drained but moisture-retentive compost

Use a fine-rosed watering-can with the rose turned upwards

**1** Fill the base of a seed pan with drainage material, then equal parts moist peat and sharp sand. Firm to within ½" (12mm) of the rim, and then add a layer of sharp sand.

**2** Lightly firm the sand and use a spatula or knife to form slits in the surface. Use tweezers to space out seeds in the grooves.

**3** Cover the seeds—without disturbing them—with coarse grit to a depth of slightly less than twice the seed's thickness. Thoroughly, but gently, water and place outdoors. Ensure that vermin and birds cannot disturb the seeds; if necessary, place wire-netting over them.

### Stratifying Seeds

This helps hard-coated seeds of trees and shrubs to germinate. Place seeds between layers of moist sand in pots and place outdoors during winter. Alternatively, place the pot in a plastic bag and put it in a refrigerator for several months. Before sowing, wash the seeds. Sow as suggested on the left.

### Advantages of Seeds

- Cheap way to raise new plants.
- Seeds rarely transmit diseases and plants are usually healthy.
- Seed-raised plants on the borderline of hardiness are more able to survive outdoors than plants raised in gentle warmth and later acclimatized to outdoor conditions.

## TAKING CUTTINGS

Many plants can be raised from cuttings, and this ensures that the progeny resembles the parent plants. There are two main types of cutting. Softwood cuttings are immature, relatively soft and taken from the current season's growth. Hardwood cuttings are formed of fully ripened wood, about one year old, and are usually taken in autumn. Softwood cuttings are usually taken in early summer, using fresh, healthy, young shoots. Hardwood cuttings are normally taken in autumn. Shown here is the technique for taking softwood cuttings of *Cryptomeria japonica* (Japanese Cedar).

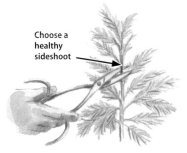

Choose a healthy sideshoot

**1** Put drainage material in the pot's base, and then firm equal parts moist peat and sharp sand to ½" (12mm) below the rim. Use scissors to sever a young, healthy stem, 2½"–3" (6–7.5cm) long.

### Looking After the Cuttings

Immediately after inserting the cuttings, carefully level the compost's surface and use a fine-rosed watering-can to water the compost from above; this helps to settle compost around the roots. Allow excess water to drain, then label the cuttings with their name as well as date.

Cuttings can be inserted in compost in seed trays as well as in pots, but if only a few cuttings are needed pots are usually better.

Place the cuttings in an unheated greenhouse or cold frame and keep the compost moderately moist, but not waterlogged. About a year later, cuttings will have developed roots and further shoots. They can then be transferred singly into small pots.

**2** Remove needles and sideshoots from the lower third of the cutting. If left, these may decay when the cutting is inserted into compost.

Use sharp scissors or a knife

**3** Use a pencil-thick dibber to insert each cutting to about one-third of its height and not nearer than ½" (12mm) to the pot's edge. Firm the compost around it.

Firm compost around the cuttings

# Pests and Diseases

## ■ Are pests and diseases a problem?

Fortunately, outdoor bonsai are hardy and usually little troubled by pests and diseases, although they do not escape completely. Indoor bonsai, with their tropical and semi-tropical origin, are more at risk, especially from leaf-sucking pests. Vigilance is essential, and when plants are watered and tended, check that there are no pests or diseases present. Before using an insecticide, check with the instructions that it is safe to use on specific plants.

## Pernicious and Ubiquitous

Outdoor bonsai are hardy and open to the pest-killing rigors of winter, which gives them a good degree of resistance to some pests and diseases. Indoor bonsai, however, have soft stems and leaves throughout the year and therefore are more likely to be attacked. The buildup of pests can be rapid.

  Not all of these pests and diseases will be seen on both outdoor and indoor bonsai but some, such as greenfly, are pernicious and have a ubiquitous nature. If left to multiply unchecked, they devastate plants.

  When getting a new plant home, always check it for signs of pests and diseases and, if necessary, isolate it while being sprayed. Plants bought from reputable bonsai nurseries are usually pest- and disease-free, but it is well worth checking them before introducing them to your collection.

*Inspect all new plants to ensure they are not infested with pests or diseases; if necessary, spray with an insecticide or fungicide. Additionally, mist-spraying keeps leaves clean and dust-free. It also helps to deter some insects. However, do not mist-spray flowers.*

### Routine Spraying

Prevention is easier than cure is the key to keeping bonsai free from pests and diseases. From early spring to late summer, spray at monthly intervals with a systemic insecticide and fungicide. Adhere to the manufacturer's instructions. Do not spray leaves that are unfolding, as they might be damaged. However, those in bud or fully open will be safe.

## DISEASES

Diseases are best prevented by regularly spraying plants. If allowed to become established, they are difficult to eradicate.

### Peach leaf curl

Peach leaf curl weakens trees (Peaches, Nectarines, and Almonds), causing damage to leaves and shoots. Reddish blisters form on leaves, later turning white. Additionally, leaves become distorted and eventually drop. Destroy affected leaves and spray with a copper fungicide.

### Powdery mildew

Powdery mildew is a fungus that grows on the surfaces of leaves, coating or spotting them with a white, powdery deposit. It is not a fatal disease, but one that is unsightly. It also spreads to stems and flowers. Spray the leaves with a systemic fungicide.

### Safety and Chemicals

Treat garden chemicals with respect.
- Before using a chemical, read the label and check that it is suitable.
- Don't use chemicals from bottles that are unlabelled.
- Always follow the manufacturer's instructions—using extra high concentrations may damage plants.
- Keep children and pets out of the way while spraying.
- Don't allow pets to chew or lick sprayed plants.
- Thoroughly clean spraying equipment after use.
- If you have an accident with a garden chemical and have to visit a doctor, take along the relevant chemical.

# PESTS AND HOW TO DEAL WITH THEM

| PEST AND SYMPTOMS | | COURSE OF ACTION |
|---|---|---|
| **Blackfly** These are related to greenfly (aphids), except that instead of being green they are black. |  | They cluster on soft stems, leaves and tender tips of shoots, sucking sap and causing considerable damage if the infestation is neglected. Additionally, when blackfly suck sap they also transmit viruses that can cause plants to deteriorate. Sometimes, leaves and shoots curl. Once spotted, eradication must be immediate. Spray with an insecticide. It may be necessary to repeat the spray several times. Regularly check for infestations. |
| **Caterpillars** Appear in spring and during early summer, when hatching from eggs. Other infestations may appear later in the year. |  | Young caterpillars feed voraciously, especially on young shoots and leaves, chewing them and causing unsightly holes. During hot, dry summers the damage is usually worse. The range of caterpillars is wide. As soon as caterpillars are noticed, pick them off and use an insecticidal spray. Additionally, where possible remove badly damaged leaves to improve the plant's appearance. Check that the compost is moist. |
| **Cuckoo spit** Also known as froghopper or common froghopper, the frothy, spit-like material covers nymphs of the froghopper. |  | Froghoppers, encapsulated by the frothy material, usually appear on the undersides of leaves and at the junctions of stems and leaves. They suck sap and cause debilitation to the plant, similar to that produced by greenfly. Additionally, leaves wilt and shoots become distorted. Remove the frothy spit by spraying with water or wiping with a damp cloth. Also, thoroughly soak the area, and the froghoppers, with an insecticide. |
| **Greenfly** Also known as aphids and aphis, this pest is green, sucks sap, transmits viruses and encourages the presence of sooty mold. |  | This widespread pest clusters in large groups around soft stems, young shoots, and on the undersides of leaves. They suck sap, causing mottling and blistering. They transmit viruses, as well as excreting a sticky substance known as honeydew, which attracts molds (usually known as sooty mold because it is black) and the presence of ants. As soon as greenfly are seen, use an insecticide. It is usually necessary to repeat the spray several times. |
| **Leaf miners** These pests, the larval stage of moths and flies, burrow into leaves and feed on their soft interiors. |  | Unfortunately, the first symptom of their presence is brown or white ribbon-like trails in leaves, causing an unsightly feature on bonsai. Certain moths and flies lay eggs on the undersides of leaves; these hatch and the young grubs enter. Spray with an insecticide as soon as damage is seen. Also, where a leaf has become unsightly, remove it entirely. |
| **Scale insects** Limpet-like, small, brown discs that attach themselves to the undersides of leaves, branches and bark. |  | Apart from looking unsightly, under their protective covering these pests suck sap, causing debilitation and, if the attack is severe, yellow and sticky honeydew which becomes a home for sooty mold. If the infestation is slight, the scales can be rubbed off by using a damp cloth or a cotton bud soaked in methylated spirit or rubbing alcohol. Additionally, spray with a systemic insecticide. Eradication is difficult and repeat spraying is necessary. |
| **Slugs and snails** These pernicious and ubiquitous pests are especially prevalent during warm, damp summers and into autumn. |  | They chew leaves, stems, and roots, causing considerable damage. For bonsai, preventing these pests reaching plants is much better than cure. They hide during the day and attack at night. Their presence can be seen by trails of slime. These pests are able, through smell, to detect the presence of soft, young shoots and leaves, so raise plants above ground level, preferably on staging. Also, put down slug baits or saucers of beer to lure them away. |
| **Vine weevils** Both adult beetles and the larvae attack plants. The beetles have thick snouts; the larvae are fat, usually curved and creamy-white. |  | Adult beetles chew and tear the leaves, while the larvae feed on roots. Attacks to leaves can be seen, but often the result of roots being chewed is not noticed for several months, when the plant wilts although the compost is moist. When repotting, check that the larvae are not present. Pick off the beetles as soon as they are seen, and spray with an insecticide. For problems with the larvae, soak the compost with an insecticide. |
| **Woolly aphids** Well-known pest and a particular problem on Beech, Cotoneasters, Pyracanthas, Hawthorns and Pines. |  | Aphid-like insects secrete masses of white, wool-like wax which smothers them. They cluster around stems and branches, causing the plant to look unsightly. Large infestations on small plants can be very debilitating. Small colonies can be removed by using a damp cloth or a cotton bud soaked in methylated spirit or rubbing alcohol. Additionally, use a winter spray, as well as an insecticide in summer, if this pest is seen. |

# Outdoor Bonsai

# Caring for Outdoor Bonsai

## ■ Is there a routine of bonsai care?

The priority in caring for outdoor bonsai is to keep the compost moist, especially from spring through early autumn. Compost that becomes dry inevitably damages roots and thereby foliage and flowers. Feeding plants during summer is also important, as the reserve of food in the small amount of compost in the plant's container is minimal. Thereafter, repotting and pruning are essential to maintain a plant's shape, size, and identity.

## Vacation Help?

There are times throughout the year when a "plant sitter" is needed to look after your bonsai. The degree of difficulty this imposes depends on the time of year; during winter a few days away may not be a problem, but in summer plants may need to be watered several times a day.

The first choice of helper is a like-minded bonsai enthusiast whom you can brief about your plants, some of which need more frequent watering than others. The next choice would be a houseplant guru with a good knowledge of plants and who is aware of their varying needs for water.

Most bonsai survive short periods when in the charge of a non-experienced waterer: even if excessively watered in summer, well-drained compost prevents long-term damage.

> ### Can I take outdoor bonsai indoors?
> This is possible, but only for short periods and if the temperature is not too high. Additionally, ensure that the compost is moist and the plant is out of strong, direct sunlight—and draughts.

*The piece of bleached driftwood looks good set against this bonsai and helps prevent it from blowing over in gusty wind.*

## Differing Needs

All plants have different needs, and bonsai are no exception. Although they all grow in containers and may appear to have the same requirements, some plants are more resilient than others. As an indication of the "toughies" and "delicates" of the bonsai world, remember that each plant's nature gives a clue to its resilience—as well as its needs.

- Evergreen conifers are some of the "toughies." Many come from cool areas, and their often needle-like leaves help to reduce their need for water when, in nature, the soil may be dry. However, they still need regular watering in summer.
- Deciduous trees and shrubs lose their leaves in autumn and overwinter as bare stems and branches. This is also one of nature's survival tactics. It is essential, however, that their compost does not become waterlogged in winter.
- Flowering trees and shrubs are not always delicate. Indeed, the winter-flowering *Hamamelis mollis* (Witch Hazel) is certainly tough. Many trees and shrubs that flower in spring are also resilient, but their flowers often arrive when the wind is frisky and sudden frosts difficult to predict. Also, a combination of rain and wind soon spoils their display. A wind-sheltered position is essential for them.

> ### Do outdoor bonsai look after themselves?
> No. They need regular care, daily, all year round. They are plants which are grown in shallow containers that hold small amounts of compost relative to the size of the plant. Watering, especially, needs vigilance if the compost is to be kept evenly moist, particularly in summer. Dry compost will kill a plant.

> ### Particularly tough bonsai
> Although evergreen conifers such as Pines survive low temperatures, they would not be so happy in extremely moist compost in which *Taxodium distichum* (Swamp Cypress) or Willows would flourish. That is not to say that either the Swamp Cypress or Willow would be comfortable in winter in exceptionally cold and continually wet compost.

# OUTDOOR BONSAI GROWING GUIDE

Making plants comfortable, according to their individual needs, requires experience, and this is part of the fascination of growing bonsai. Here are a few quick-focus pointers to looking after your plants.

Several of the topics highlighted here are also featured in detail on earlier spreads:

- Composts and their selection—pages 22–23.
- Seasonal care throughout the year—pages 24–25.
- Root-pruning and repotting—pages 28–29.
- Pruning—pages 30–31.
- Pinching—pages 32–33.
- Wiring—pages 34–35.
- Watering and feeding—pages 36–37.
- Pests and diseases—pages 40–41.

## Temperature

Outdoors, the temperature is inevitably dictated by local weather. However, it is possible to protect plants from strong, cold and gusting winds, as well as to construct a slatted canopy that reduces the intensity of strong sunlight but allows air and light to reach the plants (see pages 80–81).

- Cold winds are especially damaging in spring, when young shoots are developing and some trees and shrubs are flowering.
- High temperatures are a danger for some plants; an overhead screen is one solution, but also ensure that the compost does not become dry.

## Light

Light is essential to all plants—it activates their growth processes. In winter there is little problem from excessive sunlight, but in summer, if too strong, it may damage leaves (especially if water is allowed to fall on relatively soft leaves and act as a lens).

- Reduce strong sunlight by constructing a slatted canopy over the plants (see pages 80–81).
- Ensure plants receive sufficient light by placing them in an open position. Avoid places against walls that are in continual shade.

## Feeding

Many garden plants are not regularly fed because they are well established and their roots permeate far into the soil, but plants in shallow containers need regular feeding to ensure they develop strong, healthy growth as well as flowers (see pages 36–37).

- Fertilizers can be applied in several forms—liquid, powder, granular, or as pellets (see page 37).
- Do not increase the recommended amount of fertilizer given to a plant, as it may raise the salt concentration in the compost and make it difficult for roots to absorb water, eventually causing death.

## Watering

Water is essential to plants, but too much or too little can cause damage. The risk of damage to plants through excessive watering is greater in winter than in summer. Conversely, too little in winter causes fewer problems than too little in summer.

- When watering plants—especially those recently potted or repotted—use a watering-can with a fine rose that faces upwards (it can be rotated on the can's spout). This spreads the water and prevents compost being disturbed.
- At each watering, thoroughly soak the compost. If just the surface is dampened, the roots and lower compost may remain dry.
- Watering can be combined with feeding—see right and pages 36–37.
- Ensure that the pot is level—if uneven, water will spill over one edge and fail to soak the compost.

## Repotting

Repotting established bonsai is usually accompanied by root-pruning, which for most plants is performed every 2–3 years; this varies, however, and when they are young some plants are repotted every year. Later, this may be extended to 4–5 years.

- Most bonsai are repotted in spring or early summer (see pages 28–29 for details of root-pruning and repotting).
- Always use a clean pot that has been properly prepared to receive a bonsai (see pages 22–23).
- Use the right type of compost (see pages 22–23). Remember that some plants do not like lime in the compost; others like especially well-drained compost.

## Troubleshooting

If plants are watered and fed correctly, they are healthy and better able to survive infestations of pests than weak and sickly specimens. Some pests infest leaves and shoots; with vigilance, these can be seen at an early stage when plants are being watered and tended, and a spray used (see pages 40–41). These are pests such as greenfly, scale insects and caterpillars.

Incidentally, systemic insecticides and fungicides are ideal as they get into a plant's tissue and are better able to give protection from damage.

# A–Z of Outdoor Bonsai

## ▪ Which plants should I look for?

The range of plants for outdoor bonsai is wider than you might expect, and many of them are featured in this picture and word parade. Some plants go out of fashion, but there are many that have been stalwarts of the art of bonsai for many years and they include deciduous and evergreen trees and shrubs, as well as evergreen and deciduous conifers. Additionally, some reveal glorious flowers that bring added color to winter and spring.

## → A–Z of Deciduous Trees and Shrubs

These are popular bonsai plants and, in spring, create a colorful array of young leaves, while in autumn, many have foliage that assumes rich colors before falling. Several trees create spectacular autumnal displays, and these include *Acer buergerianum* (Trident Maple), *Fagus crenata* (Japanese Beech), and *Fagus sylvatica* (European Beech). Many other Maples are known for their autumn colors, and these look especially effective when grown as group bonsai.

Some deciduous trees are better known for their colored leaves throughout summer, and few are as attractive as cut-leaf forms of *Acer palmatum* (Japanese Maple); there are many to choose from.

Flowering deciduous trees and shrubs have great appeal, especially in spring when Japanese Cherries as well as Azaleas become drenched in color. *Malus* (Crab Apples) are other plants to seek. Fruiting trees and shrubs are further possibilities, and these include *Cotoneaster horizontalis* (Fishbone Cotoneaster).

### Getting the Name Right

Throughout this book, the latest botanical names are given, as well as earlier ones that are still used in nurseries and frequently seen in old books. This will enable plants to be correctly identified and the right plant bought when visiting nurseries.

---

### *Acer buergerianum*

**Trident Maple** (USA/UK)

Also known as *Acer trifidum*, this upright, vigorous tree creates dramatic spring and summer color, as well as rich shades of orange and red in autumn. The fresh green leaves, after unfolding in spring, have three distinct lobes. It is ideal for many styles, including root-over-rock (see pages 84–85), but not broom.

Other forms include *Acer buergerianum* 'Mino-yatsubusa' (Dwarf Trident Maple) with a diminutive nature and long leaves that in autumn assume rich red and orange shades.

**Care:**

- Repot established plants every two years in spring.
- Prune during winter and summer.
- Feed from spring to early autumn, but avoid nitrogenous fertilizers late in the season as they diminish the color intensity of autumnal leaves.
- Raise plants from seeds or cuttings.

## Acer palmatum

**Japanese Maple** (USA/UK)
An elegant, graceful tree with five-lobed (occasionally seven) leaves, which are green at first but by autumn reveal purplish or bronze hues. It can be used in most bonsai styles and is especially attractive as a specimen or in a group. Do not use in literati.

Other forms have finely dissected leaves and these include *Acer palmatum* 'Dissectum Atropurpureum' (Cut-leaf Purple Maple) with purple to bright orange leaves in autumn. Other forms include *Acer palmatum* 'Ukon' with lime-green summer leaves. There are many other forms.

**Care:**
• Repot established plants every two years.
• Prune during winter and summer.
• Feed from spring to early autumn, but for plants grown for their autumnal colors avoid nitrogenous fertilizers late in the season.
• Raise new plants from seeds, although forms of it must be raised from cuttings or layers.

## Acer pseudoplatanus

**False Plane** (UK) **Mock Plane** (USA) **Sycamore** (USA/UK) **Sycamore Maple** (USA)
Vigorous tree with large leaves, usually formed of five leaves but sometimes reduced to three on bonsai. Attractive, pale, grayish bark that peels in large, irregular flakes. Because of its relatively large leaves, it is best grown as a specimen bonsai, rather than forming a group with others.

**Care:**
• Repot established plants every 1–2 years. This helps to restrain the tree's growth.
• Prune in winter, as well as reducing the number of buds. Also, removing all of the leaves in early summer reduces the leaf size.
• Feed from spring to early autumn to encourage new growth.
• Raise new plants from seeds. Additionally, use young seedlings (with permission) from the wild.

## Acer rubrum

**Red Maple** (USA/UK) **Scarlet Maple** (USA) **Soft Maple** (USA) **Swamp Maple** (USA)
Naturally forms a rounded head of three- or five-lobed leaves, dark green above and blue-white beneath. The middle lobe is the largest. The bark is grayish and shiny, except when young. It is ideal as a single tree, or in a group.

Other forms have especially attractive leaves in autumn; these include *Acer rubrum* 'Schlesingeri'.

**Care:**
• Repot established plants every two years.
• Prune during winter and summer.
• Feed from spring to early autumn, but avoid nitrogenous fertilizers late in the season.
• Raise new plants from seeds, although forms of it must be raised from cuttings or layers.

## Aesculus hippocastanum

**Common Horse Chestnut** (USA/UK) **European Horse Chestnut** (USA)
Large tree with a rounded head and large, distinctive leaves formed of five to seven leaflets. Additionally, it develops tall candles of flowers, followed by the popular mahogany-brown, shiny, conkers (seeds).

**Care:**
• Repot every 1–2 years.
• Prune in winter, as well as reducing the number of buds. Additionally, by removing all of the leaves in early summer the size of the leaves can be reduced.
• Feed from spring to early autumn to encourage new growth, especially in early and mid-summer.
• Raise new plants from seeds or seedlings taken (with permission) from the wild.

## Betula nana

**Arctic Birch** (UK) **Dwarf Birch** (USA/UK)
Dwarf and neat bush, with erect branches clothed in delicate twigs and rounded, dark green leaves. The shrub's bark is especially attractive—coppery and shiny.

Its upright nature makes it suitable for several styles, including root-over-rock, broom, informal upright and slanting, and in a group.

**Care:**
- Repot every two years.
- Prune in winter—cut out crossing shoots and try to keep the plant neat and compact. Throughout summer, trim back young shoots to one or two leaves.
- Feed from late spring to late summer.
- Raise plants from softwood cuttings taken in late spring and summer.

## Betula pendula

**European White Birch** (USA)
**Silver Birch** (UK) **White Birch** (USA)
Distinctive, broadly oval to diamond-shaped green leaves that assume shades of clear yellow in autumn. The branches tend to be pendulous towards their ends. The bark is silvery-white and is especially attractive in winter when caught by low rays of the sun.

There are several beautiful forms of this tree, including *Betula pendula* 'Dalecarlica' (Swedish Cut-leaf Birch) which has pendulous branches.

It is ideal for planting in a group or in an upright style with twin trunks.

**Care:**
- Repot every two years.
- Prune in winter and young shoots in spring, cutting them back to 2–3 leaves. Additionally, removing all leaves in early summer encourages branching.
- Feed from late spring to late summer.
- Raise new plants from seeds.

## Carpinus turczaninowii

**Korean Hornbeam** (UK)
Small, graceful, shrubby, deciduous tree with small, oval, green leaves that assume rich orange-red shades in autumn before falling.

Other species include *Carpinus betulus* (Common Beech or European Beech), which has a large, pyramidal nature and stripped and ridged gray bark. The mid-green leaves have serrated edges and in autumn they assume attractive shades of yellow.

It is ideal for many styles, including groups.

**Care:**
- Repot plants every two years.
- Prune in winter, and trim new shoots to one or two leaves in spring and early summer.
- Feed from spring to late summer.
- Raise new plants from seeds, or softwood cuttings during mid-summer.

## Cercidiphyllum japonicum

**Katsura Tree** (USA/UK)
Beautiful tree, with spirally twisted, furrowed bark. The rounded and tooth-edged leaves are red when unfolding, but soon become rich green. In autumn, they assume rich red and yellow shades. Slightly acid soil produces good autumn color. Unfortunately, leaves are easily damaged by dry compost, as well as by strong, cold wind in spring.

It is ideal for bonsai styles such as informal upright, cascading, slanting, broom and groups.

**Care:**
- Repot every 2–3 years.
- Prune in winter and trim back young growth throughout summer.
- Feed throughout summer, but not in autumn.
- Raise new plants from seeds, cuttings and layers.

## Cornus officinalis

**Japanese Cornelian Cherry** (USA/UK) **Japanese Cornel** (USA)

Hardy, deciduous small tree or shrub with lustrous, oval, mid-green leaves that create a dominant canopy. In autumn, they assume rich shades of red before falling. However, in early spring, it bears clusters of yellow flowers on bare stems, followed by red fruits.

It is ideal for several styles, including informal upright, slanting, cascade and semi-cascade, root-over-rock, and in a group.

Other species suitable for bonsai include *Cornus kousa* (Kousa, Flowering Dogwood) with narrowly oval dark green leaves that turn rich brown and red in autumn. Additionally, it has white flowers in early summer.

*Care:*
• Repot every two years.
• Prune after the flowers fade in spring.
• Feed from mid-spring to late summer.
• Raise new plants by layering and sowing seeds.

## Euonymus alatus

**Winged Spindle Tree** (USA/UK)

Slow-growing, with an upright, stiff stance, and oval to pear-shaped dark green leaves that turn crimson to rose-scarlet in autumn. Insignificant flowers appear in early summer, followed by purple fruits that contain scarlet seeds.

Other forms include *Euonymus alatus* 'Compactus', with a dense, low-growing nature.

It can be trained into all styles, except broom.

*Care:*
• Repot young plants every year, then every two years when mature.
• Prune in winter; in spring or early summer cut all new shoots back to two or three leaves.
• Feed from late spring to late summer.
• Raise new plants from hardwood cuttings in autumn or early winter, or by softwood cuttings in summer. Layering is another possibility.

## Fagus sylvatica

**Common Beech** (UK)
**European Beech** (USA)

Large, slow-growing tree with smooth, gray bark and silky-textured, oval, and serrated green leaves that in autumn assume rich golden tints.

There are several forms, including *Fagus sylvatica* 'Atropurpurea' with purple-red leaves. Additionally, some forms have cut leaves, and these are best displayed as individual bonsai, rather than in a group.

The species is ideal for formal and informal upright styles, as well as slanting and group displays.

*Care:*
• Repot every two years, especially when the plant is young.
• Prune in winter, and in spring, pinch back growing tips to two leaves.
• Feed from spring to late summer. However, remember that nitrogenous fertilizers often reduce the display of autumn color.
• Raise new plants from seeds.

## Morus alba

**White Mulberry** (USA/UK)

Slow-growing tree with a rounded head and broadly oval to heart-shaped lightish green, coarsely tooth-edged and sometimes three-lobed leaves. The rough and gnarled bark creates an attractive feature. Incidentally, this is the tree that for thousands of years the Chinese grew for its leaves, which were used to feed silkworms; but it is *Morus nigra* (Black Mulberry) that is grown for edible fruits.

It is ideal for an informal upright style, as well as slanting and semi-cascading. It also suits the root-over-rock style.

*Care:*
• Repot every two years.
• Prune in winter, as well as trimming back new growth to two leaves.
• Feed from spring to late summer.
• Raise new plants from seeds or cuttings in spring.

## Platanus x hispanica

**London Plane Tree** (USA/UK)
Also known as *Platanus acerifolia*, this splendid, large, round-headed tree, with an erect trunk, has characteristic bark that peels off in large flakes. It has lobed leaves, which are mid-green when young.

It is ideal for informal and upright styles of bonsai.

**Care:**
- Repot every 2–3 years.
- Prune in winter, and pinch back young shoots as they develop.
- Feed from spring to late summer.
- Raise new plants from seeds (but germination is sparse and the resultant seedlings may not resemble the parent). Alternatively, raise from hardwood cuttings.

## Quercus cerris

**Turkey Oak** (USA/UK)
Hardy, deciduous, fast-growing tree with a rounded head of mid- to dark green, oval to oblong, sharply lobed leaves that in autumn become bronze before falling. With age, the tree's head tends to spread.

It is especially suited to informal upright slanting and group bonsai.

**Care:**
- Repot young trees annually; later every 2–3 years.
- Prune during winter, in spring and early summer trim new shoots to one or two leaves.
- Feed throughout summer and into early autumn.
- Raise new plants from acorns.

## Quercus palustris

**Pin Oak** (USA/UK)
**Spanish Oak** (USA)
Hardy, lofty, deciduous tree with slender branches and large leaves with five or seven sharply pointed lobes. Initially they are bright green, later darker and assuming rich scarlet shades in autumn. Indeed, bonsai specimens usually create a more reliable autumn display of color than trees growing in the wild.

It is especially suited to informal upright slanting and group bonsai.

**Care:**
- Repot young trees annually; later every 2–3 years.
- Prune during winter; in spring and early summer, trim new shoots to one or two leaves.
- Feed throughout summer and into early autumn.
- Raise new plants from acorns.

## Quercus robur

**Common Oak** (UK) **English Oak** (USA/UK) **Pedunculate Oak** (UK) **Truffle Oak** (USA)
Robust, slow-growing, and large-headed tree with short-stalked, severally lobed leaves. In spring, they are bright green, slowly changing to mid- and dark green, then in autumn they assume a rich, bronze-gold. Eventually, the trunk becomes rugged and thick.

It is especially suited to informal upright, slanting, and group bonsai.

**Care:**
- Repot young trees annually; later every 2–3 years.
- Prune during winter, and during spring and early summer, trim new shoots to 1–2 leaves.
- Feed throughout summer and into early autumn.
- Raise new plants from acorns.

## Robinia pseudoacacia

**Black Locust** (USA/UK)
**Common Acacia** (UK)
**False Acacia** (USA/UK)
**Yellow Acacia** (USA)
Hardy, graceful, deciduous tree with deeply furrowed rough bark and leaves formed of many light green leaflets. Additionally, in early summer, it bears pendulous clusters of fragrant, creamy-white leaves.

The form *Robinia pseudoacacia* 'Frisia' has leaves which are golden-yellow in spring and later turn pale greenish-yellow.

It is ideal for informal upright, slanting, semi-cascade and group styles.

**Care:**
- Repot every two years.
- Prune new growth throughout summer in order to create an attractive shape.
- Feed from late spring to late summer.
- Raise new plants from cuttings or seeds and by layering.

## Salix babylonica

**Weeping Willow** (USA/UK)
Vigorous, fast-growing, graceful tree, initially with an upward nature and later revealing pendent branches bearing slender, narrow, lance-shaped, pale to mid-green leaves. It also displays greenish-yellow catkins.

It is ideal for forming informal upright, slanting, cascade and root-over-rock styles.

**Care:**
- Repot more frequently than normal: twice a year in early spring and mid-summer.
- Prune twice a year, cutting back young growth to encourage the development of young shoots.
- Feed every two weeks from early spring to late summer. Feeding too late in the season encourages unnecessary growth.
- Raise new plants from softwood cuttings in late spring or early summer, and hardwood cuttings in autumn.

## Sophora japonica

**Chinese Scholar Tree** (USA) **Japanese Pagoda Tree** (USA/UK)
**Pagoda Tree** (USA/UK)
Round-headed tree, usually with a tall trunk revealing bark that becomes gray with age and corrugated like an ash. The mid-green leaves are formed of 9–15 leaflets. In late summer and early autumn, old trees produce creamy-white, pea-type flowers in drooping clusters. It is an ideal bonsai for creating late flowers.

It is ideal for several bonsai styles, including informal upright, slanting, cascade and groups.

**Care:**
- Repot every 1–2 years.
- Prune in winter, as well as trimming young growth to maintain a neat outline.
- Feed from spring to late summer.
- Raise plants from seeds and cuttings.

## Sorbus aucuparia

**Common Rowan** (UK) **European Mountain Ash** (USA) **Mountain Ash** (UK)
**Quickbeam** (USA) **Rowan** (USA/UK)
Initially upright, then spreading, highly decorative tree with leaves formed of 6–7 pairs of oval, serrated leaflets. They reveal a fresh greenness throughout summer, while in autumn assume rich shades of orange and gold. It also bears white flowers in late spring and early summer, followed in late summer by clusters of globular, orange-red berries.

It is suitable for most bonsai styles, except broom and formal upright.

**Care:**
- Repot every 1–2 years.
- Prune in winter, as well as trimming back shoots to 1–2 leaves during early summer.
- Feed from late spring to late summer.
- Raise new plants from seeds (although plants may be variable).

## Sorbus cashmiriana

**Cashmiriana Mountain Ash** (UK)
Hardy, deciduous, small and rather loosely branched tree with dark green leaves usually formed of 6–9 pairs of leaflets. Their upper surfaces are an attractive rich green, while the undersides are gray-green. Additionally, during late spring, it bears pendulous clusters of pale pink flowers.

It is ideal for most styles, except broom and formal upright.

**Care:**
- Repot every 1–2 years.
- Prune in winter, as well as trimming back shoots to 1–2 leaves during early summer.
- Feed from late spring to late summer.
- Raise new plants from seeds (although plants may be variable).

## Stewartia pseudocamellia

**Japanese Stewartia** (USA)
Distinctive tree with flaking bark and mid-green, oval leaves that in autumn assume rich shades of yellow and red. The species name is a reference to the somewhat Camellia-like single flowers. These cup-shaped, white flowers appear during mid and late summer. It is a lime-hating tree and needs to be given acid potting compost.

It is ideal for growing in a formal style or in a group, when it is especially attractive in autumn.

*Care:*
• Repot every two years, using lime-free compost.
• Prune in winter, as well as trimming new growth to 1–2 leaves.
• Feed from spring to late summer, using an ericaceous fertilizer.
• Raise new plants by seeds and by softwood cuttings in early summer.

## Tilia cordata

**Small-leaved European Lime** (USA)
**Small-leaved Lime** (UK)
Also known as *Tilia parvifolia*, this small-leaved lime is ideal for bonsai. It has smooth, gray bark and rounded to heart-shaped, finely tooth-edged, lime-green leaves. In mid-summer it produces fragrant, small, bowl-shaped, yellow-white flowers in small, pendulous clusters. Regularly check that greenfly are not present on young shoots and leaves.

It is ideal for most styles of bonsai, especially informal displays. Do not use it for literati.

*Care:*
• Repot every year when young; later every two years.
• Prune in winter, and regularly throughout summer to maintain the plant's shape.
• Feed from late spring to late summer.
• Raise new plants from seeds and softwood cuttings in early summer.

## Ulmus glabra

**Scotch Elm** (USA/UK)
**Wych Elm** (USA/UK)
Hardy, lofty and dominant deciduous tree with a head of wide-spreading branches, eventually more dome-shaped, and gray-brown bark. The oval to pear-shaped leaves are slender, pointed, and coarsely tooth-edged. In autumn, these dull-green leaves become yellow.

It is ideal for creating most styles.

*Care:*
• Repot annually when young; later as necessary.
• Prune in winter, as well as trimming new shoots throughout summer.
• Feed from spring to late summer.
• Raise new plants from cuttings and by grafts.

## Ulmus x hollandica 'Jacqueline Hillier'

Earlier known as *Ulmus* x *elegantissima* 'Jacqueline Hillier', this hardy, small, suckering, deciduous shrubby tree has a dense but neat nature and slender brown twigs that are clothed in small, double-tooth-edged, mid- to dark green leaves.

All specimens originate from a plant found in the Midlands in Britain many years ago.

It is ideal for creating most styles.

*Care:*
• Repot annually when young; later as necessary.
• Prune in winter, as well as trimming new shoots throughout summer.
• Feed from spring to late summer.
• Raise new plants from cuttings and by grafts.

## Ulmus parvifolia

**Chinese Elm** (USA/UK)
**Leather-leaf Elm** (USA)
Slender trunk, with a rounded head and slender branches. The somewhat leathery, oval to pear-shaped leaves are tooth-edged and lustrous green.

It is ideal for most styles of bonsai, including clasped-to-rock and broom. Indeed, its slender, almost twiggy branches are ideal for the broom style.

*Care:*
• Repot every year when young; later as necessary.
• Prune in winter, as well as trimming new shoots throughout spring and summer.
• Feed from late spring to late summer or early autumn.
• Raise plants from softwood or hardwood cuttings.

## Ulmus procera

**English Elm** (USA/UK)
Also known as *Ulmus campestris*, it has an erect nature and broadly oval, mid- to deep green, serrated leaves that in autumn assume clear yellow shades. The gray-brown bark is attractive and, with age, becomes increasingly fissured. When grown as a bonsai, the leaves are smaller than in the wild.

It is ideal for creating most styles, especially informal ones.

*Care:*
• Repot annually when young. When mature—after about ten years—repot as necessary.
• Prune in winter; in spring trim shoots to two sets of leaves. It can also be leaf-pruned in mid-summer.
• Feed from spring to late summer.
• Raise new plants from softwood and hardwood cuttings.

## Zelkova serrata

**Japanese Elm** (USA/UK)
**Japanese Zelkova** (USA) **Saw-leaf Zelkova** (USA)
Tall tree with smooth, gray bark and long, erect branches. The oval to lance-shaped, dark green leaves taper and reveal serrated edges; in autumn they gradually change through crimson and bronze to orange and yellow.

It is ideal for most styles, and is especially attractive when in a group. Do not use it for the literati style.

*Care:*
• Repot annually when the plant is young, but after about ten years extend this to every two years.
• Prune during winter; in spring and early summer trim back new shoots to 1–2 leaves. To maintain the plant's diminutive nature, regularly remove large leaves.
• Feed from late spring to the early part of late summer; high nitrogenous fertilizers in late summer reduce autumnal displays.
• Raise new plants from seeds and softwood cuttings during summer.

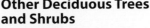

## Other Deciduous Trees and Shrubs
• *Acer campestre*
• *Acer ginnala*
• *Caragana arborescens*
• *Carpinus laxiflora*
• *Crataegus laevigata*
• *Enkianthus campanulatus*
• *Fagus crenata*
• *Gleditsia triacanthos*
• *Nothofagus antarctica*
• *Nothofagus obliqua*
• *Nothofagus procera*
• *Populus alba*
• *Populus nigra*

## Evergreen Shrubs and Trees
• *Buxus microphylla*
• *Buxus sempervirens*
• *Elaeagnus multiflora*
• *Elaeagnus pungens*
• *Ilex crenata*
• *Ligustrum ovalifolium*
• *Ligustrum vulgare*
• *Lonicera nitida*
• *Myrtus communis*
• *Osmanthus delavayi*

# → A–Z of Conifers (Deciduous and Evergreen)

Conifers have a dignified nature and radiate an aura of permanency, and so are ideal for creating interest in a bonsai collection throughout the year. The majority of conifers are evergreen; a few are deciduous, and although bare of foliage throughout winter, they more than compensate for this by revealing fresh, young growth in spring. Some have leaves that assume rich colors in autumn, before falling.

The range of evergreen conifers is wide, from *Pinus* (Pines) to *Picea* (Spruces), *Juniperus* (Junipers), and *Tsuga* (Hemlocks). Deciduous conifers include *Ginkgo biloba* (Maidenhair Tree), *Larix decidua* (European Larch), *Taxodium distichum* (Swamp Cypress), and *Metasequoia glyptostroboides* (Dawn Redwood).

When planning a display of coniferous bonsai, have both evergreen and deciduous types and intersperse them throughout the other plants. Some evergreen conifers are ideal for cascades and other styles, while deciduous types are better on their own or as groups in the same container.

## Timeless Trees

Historically, conifers are age-old trees and members of a group of primitive, cone-bearing plants; it is this quality that gives them a timeless nature. However, some conifers, such as the well-known and popular *Taxus baccata* (Yew) and *Ginkgo biloba* (Maidenhair Tree), do not bear cones.

## Cedrus libani

**Cedar of Lebanon** (USA/UK)
Large, slow-growing, distinctive evergreen conifer, pyramidal when young and later spreading. It develops a flat top and layers of horizontal branches bearing dark green, needle-like leaves. It also bears barrel-shaped cones. Native to the Near East and, historically famed in the Lebanon, it forms vast forests in the Taurus range of mountains in southern Turkey. It is ideal for both formal and informal styles, preferably on its own so that the beautifully layered branches can be clearly seen.
***Care:*** • Repot every 3–4 years. • Prune in spring, pinching back new shoots, but not damaging the needles. • Feed from late spring to late summer. • Raise new plants from seeds, as well as hardwood cuttings in late summer and early autumn.

## Chamaecyparis obtusa

**Hinoki Cypress** (USA/UK)
**Hinoki False Cypress** (USA)
**Japanese False Cypress** (USA)
Slow-growing, evergreen conifer with a broadly conical outline and reddish-brown bark with shallow fissures. The scale-like, somewhat boat-like, bright green leaves have silvery-white marks on their undersides and when bruised reveal a warm, sweet bouquet reminiscent of pencils.

There are many forms, including the semi-dwarf *Chamaecyparis obtusa* 'Nana Gracilis', with shiny green leaves.

It is ideal for most styles of bonsai, except broom.
**Care:**
• Repot every other year when the plant is young, then each time roots fill the container.
• Prune by pinching out the tips of foliage during the growing season.
• Feed from late spring to late autumn.
• Raise new plants from softwood as well as hardwood cuttings.

## Chamaecyparis pisifera

**Sarawa Cypress** (USA/UK)
Distinctive evergreen conifer with a conical outline; in the wild it reveals a nodding leading shoot. The bright reddish-brown bark has distinctive parallel ridges. The bright green foliage appears in fern-like sprays and when bruised has a resinous bouquet.

There are many attractive forms, including *Chamaecyparis pisifera* 'Boulevard' (Blue Moss Cypress) with bright bluish-silver and green, feathery foliage. *Chamaecyparis pisifera* 'Plumosa' initially has a conical outline, later columnar, with bright green somewhat fluffy-ended foliage.

It is ideal for many styles, such as informal upright, slanting and group.
**Care:**
• Repot every other year when young, but later when roots fill the container.
• Prune by pinching out the tips of foliage during the growing season.
• Feed from late spring to late autumn.
• Raise new plants from softwood as well as hardwood cuttings.

## Cryptomeria japonica

**Japanese Cedar** (USA/UK) **Japanese Red Cedar** (UK)
Moderately fast-growing evergreen conifer with bright, orange-brown, peeling bark and needle-like, bright blue-green, curved and dagger-shaped leaves. In the wild, the foliage is borne in either long, sparse clusters or dense, short bunches.

Other forms include *Cryptomeria japonica* 'Tansu', also known as *C. japonica* 'Yatsubusa', a dwarf form with a narrow, conical nature and compact foliage.

It is ideal for most styles and especially informal upright, group, and clasped-to-rock.

**Care:**
• Repot every other year when young, but later extend this to every 4–6 years.
• Prune throughout summer by pinching back new shoots.
• Feed from mid-spring to late autumn.
• Raise new plants from softwood cuttings.

## Ginkgo biloba

**Maidenhair Tree** (USA/UK)
Beautiful, slow-growing, deciduous conifer with distinctive, fan-shaped, nearly two-lobed, leathery, fresh green leaves in spring that change during summer to mid-green then, in autumn, to pale yellow. The fissured, dark gray bark is especially attractive in winter. Trees vary in shape: males have a pyramidal nature, whereas female ones in Europe are tall and narrow.

It is suited to both upright and group styles.

**Care:**
• Repot annually during its early years, but later every 2–3 years.
• Prune with great care, as it resents large cuts—they may not heal. During the growing season, use sharp scissors to cut back young shoots to two or three leaves.
• Feed from spring to mid-summer.
• Raise new plants from seeds or hardwood cuttings in late summer or early autumn.

## Juniperus chinensis

**Chinese Juniper** (USA/UK)
A shrub or tree with a deciduous nature and narrow, broadly conical outline and pale, reddish-brown, stringy bark. The juvenile leaves are awl-shaped, while adult ones are scale-like and dull, dark green.

Other forms include dwarf types as well as others with golden foliage.

It is ideal for most styles of bonsai, except broom.

**Care:**
• Repot every 2–3 years.
• Prune during late spring or late summer; pinch back young shoots.
• Feed from late spring to late summer.
• Raise new plants from cuttings.

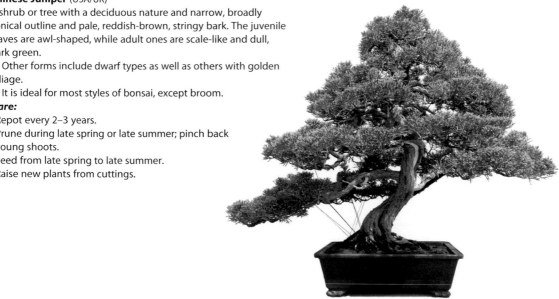

## Larix decidua

**Common Larch** (UK)
**European Larch** (USA/UK)
Beautiful, graceful and elegant, deciduous conifer with an upright nature and tapering trunk with scaly bark and pale yellowish-gray branches. The bright green, narrow leaves become golden or russet in autumn.

It is ideal for many styles of bonsai, including upright and groups. However, it is not suitable for a broom display.

**Care:**
- Repot annually in spring.
- Prune in winter to shape it, but in summer pinch back new growth.
- Feed from late spring to late summer, but not into autumn.
- Raise new plants from seeds, as well as cuttings in late spring and early autumn.

## Larix kaempferi

**Japanese Larch** (USA/UK)
Also known as *Larix leptolepis*, this deciduous, relatively fast-growing larch has a wide-spreading head and scaling bark that reveals pale, gray-brown underbark. Branches are dark red or reddish-brown and have a gray bloom during their first winter. It bears short, glaucous, or gray-green needles which, in autumn, assume shades of pale yellow.

It is ideal for most styles of bonsai, except broom.

**Care:**
- Repot every year in spring.
- Prune in winter; additionally, throughout summer, pinch back new shoots.
- Feed from late spring to late summer, but not into autumn.
- Raise new plants from seeds, as well as from cuttings in late summer or early autumn.

## Metasequoia glyptostroboides

**Dawn Redwood** (USA/UK) **Water Fir** (UK)
Tall, majestic, deciduous conifer with cinnamon-colored or dark gray fissured bark that peels on old trees. The light green, flattened but somewhat needle-like leaves turn a glorious red-brown in autumn before falling. It is a well-known conifer, originally known only through fossils; living trees were first seen by a Chinese botanist in 1941, while seeds were collected in 1947.

It is ideal for both formal and informal upright styles, as well as clump and slanting.

**Care:**
- Repot every other year, in spring.
- Prune in summer by trimming back new shoots.
- Feed from late spring to late summer, but not into autumn.
- Raise plants from seeds and cuttings.

## Picea abies

**Common Spruce** (UK)
**Norway Spruce** (USA/UK)
Distinctive, hardy evergreen conifer with a narrow spire when young but becoming broad and domed. When young, the orange-brown bark flakes and later cracks and changes, in part, to dark purple-gray. The shoots are reddish-brown and the short, flattened needle-like leaves are dark green.

It is often grown in its dwarf forms, such as 'Little Gem' and 'Maxwellii'.

It is ideal for most bonsai styles, except broom.

**Care:**
- Repot every other year, in spring. Later this can be extended to every 4–5 years.
- Prune during spring and summer by pinching back young shoots.
- Feed from spring to mid-autumn.
- Raise plants from seeds or cuttings.

## *Picea glauca* var. *albertana* 'Conica'

Sometimes listed and sold as *Picea glauca* 'Albertana Conica', this slow-growing and dwarf form of the white or Canadian spruce has an evergreen nature and compact, conical outline. It becomes smothered in grass-green leaves. It is said to be derived from a plant that was found in Alberta, Canada, in 1904.

It is ideal for formal upright styles, as well as group displays. Do not use it for the broom style.

**Care:**
- Repot every other year when young; with maturity, this can be extended to every five years.
- Prune during spring and summer, pinch off young shoots to about two-thirds of their length.
- Feed from late spring to early autumn.
- Raise new plants from seeds or softwood cuttings.

## *Picea jezoensis*

**Edo Spruce** (UK)
**Yezo Spruce** (UK)
**Yeddo Spruce** (USA)
Hardy evergreen conifer with shiny, pale brown to yellowish-brown young shoots and densely crowded, flattened, needle-like leaves. These are glossy and dark green above, and silvery-white beneath.

It is also grown in the form *Picea jezoensis* subsp. *hondoensis* (Hondo Spruce). It has short needle-like leaves, which are dull green above.

It is ideal for most styles of bonsai, except broom.

**Care:**
- Repot every other year, in spring. Later this can be extended to every 4–5 years.
- Prune during spring and summer, by pinching back young shoots.
- Feed from spring to mid-autumn.
- Raise plants from seeds or cuttings.

## *Pinus parviflora*

**Japanese White Pine** (USA/UK)
Also known as *Pinus pentaphylla*, this evergreen conifer develops a low crown and wide-spreading branches. The purple bark is attractive, with patches of black scales. The blue-white needles are borne in groups of five.

There are many forms, including *Pinus parviflora* 'Kokonoe' (Dwarf Japanese White Pine).

The species is ideal for many styles of bonsai, except broom.

**Care:**
- Repot every 2–5 years.
- Prune in spring, pinching off about one-third of each new shoot.
- Feed from late spring to late autumn.
- Raise new plants from seeds.

## Pinus sylvestris

**Scotch Fir** (USA/UK) **Scotch Pine** (USA)
**Scots Pine** (USA/UK)
Distinctive evergreen conifer, often with
a wild, windswept and aged appearance.
Young trees have conical crowns, but with
age, they spread and become irregular.
The gray-green needles are borne in pairs.

There are several forms used in
bonsai, and these include *Pinus sylvestris*
'Beauvronensis' (Dwarf Scots Pine), which
is dwarf and slow-growing.

The species is ideal for most styles
including literati, but not broom.
**Care:**
• Repot every 2–5 years.
• Prune during summer by trimming off
  about one-third to a half of the candles.
  In late summer, remove old needles and
  cut out crowded twigs.
• Feed from spring to mid- or late autumn.
• Raise new plants by seeds. Dwarf forms
  are usually grafted.

## Sequoia sempervirens

**California Redwood** (UK) **Coast Redwood**
(USA) **Coastal Redwood** (USA/UK)
**Redwood** (USA)
Immensely tall, evergreen conifer with
a columnar nature, although the lower
branches curve and sweep downward.
The rich, brown-red bark has an attractive,
fibrous nature, while the flattened, needle-
like leaves vary; they are mid-green and
curved on main shoots and dark green,
flat, and narrow on lateral ones.

It is ideal for formal and informal
upright styles, as well as for slanting and
group.
**Care:**
• Repot every 3–4 years.
• Prune during summer, shortening the
  new growth to maintain a desired shape.
• Feed from late spring to late summer.
• Raise plants from seeds or cuttings.

## Sequoiadendron giganteum

**Big Tree** (USA)
**California Redwood** (USA/UK)
**Giant Redwood** (USA/UK)
**Giant Sequoia** (USA)
**Mammoth Tre**e (UK)
**Sierra Redwood** (UK)
Earlier known as *Sequoia gigantea*, this
hardy, gigantic, evergreen conifer has a
conical outline and drooping branches.
The tree has attractive, red-brown, fibrous,
and spongy bark and dark green, awl-
shaped leaves. When bruised, they have an
aromatic fragrance.

It is ideal for formal and informal
upright styles, as well as for slanting and
group.
**Care:**
• Repot every 3–4 years.
• Prune during summer, shortening the
  new growth to maintain a desired shape.
• Feed from late spring to late summer.
• Raise plants from seeds or cuttings.

## Taxodium distichum

**Bald Cypress** (USA/UK) **Swamp Cypress**
(UK)
Distinctive, long-lived, deciduous conifer
with fibrous, pale reddish-brown, closely
ridged bark. The narrow, bright yellow-
green leaves are borne in two flattened
rows. During autumn, they first turn fox-
red, then orange, before falling.

It is suitable for many styles, including
formal and informal upright, slanting and
in a group. It is also ideal for clasped-to-
rock style.
**Care:**
• Repot every other year.
• Prune by pinching out young shoots
  during late spring and summer.
• Feed from late spring to late summer.
• Raise new plants from seeds and cuttings.

## *Taxus baccata*

**Common Yew** (UK) **English Yew** (USA/UK)
Slow-growing, broad, well-branched, evergreen conifer with red-brown peeling bark. The narrow, stiff and sharp leaves are dark and glossy, almost black-green above and a gray, pale green below. The foliage and berries are poisonous to children, adults, and animals.

It is suitable for most styles of bonsai, but not broom.

*Care:*
- Repot every 3–4 years—and sometimes more.
- Prune during summer, pinching out new shoots to encourage branching, and to produce a neat outline.
- Feed from late spring to late summer.
- Raise new plants from cuttings in late summer or early autumn, taken from current season's growth.

## *Tsuga canadensis*

**Eastern Hemlock** (UK)
**Canada Hemlock** (USA)
Hardy, evergreen conifer, often with several stems and a bushy nature, with dark gray-brown, roughly ridged bark and dark green, small, narrow, and somewhat needle-like leaves.

It is ideal for most styles of bonsai, except broom.

*Care:*
- Repot every two years when young, later extending this time to 3–4 years for mature plants.
- Prune during summer, pinching out new shoots and leaving just a few needles.
- Feed from late spring to early autumn.
- Raise new plants from cuttings, as well as sowing seeds.

## *Tsuga heterophylla*

**Western Hemlock** (USA/UK)
A tall, slender, and elegant evergreen conifer with a pyramidal outline and branches that display slightly drooping ends. The short, needle-like, fresh green leaves that hang from the branches mature to an attractive dark green. The trunk has dark brown bark, furrowed in scaly ridges.

It is suitable for most styles of bonsai, except broom.

*Care:*
- Repot every two years when young, later extending this time to 3–4 years for mature plants.
- Prune during summer, pinching out new shoots and leaving just a few needles.
- Feed from late spring to early autumn.
- Raise new plants from seeds and softwood cuttings in summer.

### Other Evergreen Conifers
- *Abies alba*
- *Abies koreana*
- *Abies lasiocarpa*
- *Abies lasiocarpa* var. *arizonica*
- *Abies lasiocarpa* var. *arizonica* 'Compacta'
- *Cedrus atlantica*
- *Cedrus atlantica* 'Glauca'
- *Cedrus brevifolia*
- *Juniperus communis*
- *Juniperus procumbens*
- *Juniperus rigida*
- *Juniperus sabina*
- *Picea jezoensis*
- *Taxus cuspidata*
- *Tsuga canadensis*

# ➡ A–Z of Flowering Trees and Shrubs

Flowering bonsai always create excitement, especially in winter and spring when the area may be bare of color. The range of flowering bonsai is wide and encompasses both deciduous and evergreen shrubs and trees, as well as climbers such as the glorious Wisteria.

Few trees epitomize spring as much as Cherry trees and other *Prunus* species. *Prunus* 'Kanzan', earlier widely planted to decorate street verges in towns, creates a wealth of double, light purple-pink flowers during the latter half of mid-spring, while *Prunus padus* 'Watereri' (Bird Cherry) has drooping tassels packed with almond-scented flowers. Forsythia is popular for its early and mid-spring, rich yellow flowers which festoon bare stems. For clusters of golden-yellow flowers, try *Forsythia* x *intermedia*. Lilac is another revelation in spring; for bonsai, the best is the *Syringa meyeri* var. *spontanea* 'Palibin', also known as *Syringa palibiniana*.

## Single or Massed?

Many flowering bonsai have displays formed of massed flowers, but some reveal single flowers. These include Camellias, which are well known for their late-winter and spring flowers. The attention-seeking *Magnolia stellata* (Star Magnolia) also has large, single flowers.

## Azalea indica

Properly known as *Rhododendron indicum* but still widely known as Azaleas, Satsuki Azaleas are evergreen and create magnificent displays in early summer. They are ideal as bonsai and have smallish, dark green, narrow leaves that cluster along short stems. The color range is wide and includes white, pink, red, and purple. Kurume Azaleas, derived from *Rhododendron kiusianum*, can also be grown as bonsai but are not so popular or as flamboyant as Satsuki types.

These Azaleas are soon damaged by frost and a wind-sheltered position is needed.

### Care:

- Repot annually or when roots fill the pot. Wait until the flowers fade. Use lime-free compost.
- Prune by removing flowers as soon as they fade. Additionally, pinch out new shoots; this will encourage the development of further ones.
- Feed in early spring, before flowering, and again afterwards and until mid-autumn.
- Raise new plants from softwood cuttings taken in early summer.

## Chaenomeles japonica

**Cydonia** (UK) **Flowering Quince** (USA/UK)
**Japanese Quince** (UK)

Distinctive, deciduous shrub with a wide-spreading nature and oval to round, mid-green leaves. It produces orange-red, apple-blossom-like flowers in clusters of two or three on the previous season's growth over a long period in spring and into early summer. As a bonsai, it creates a magnificent display.

It is ideal for many styles of bonsai, except broom and formal upright.

**Care:**
• Repot every 2–3 years.
• Prune in autumn, cut back the current season's growth to two joints. Do not prune in spring, as this will decrease the plant's flowering ability.
• Feed from when flowering ceases to mid- or late autumn.
• Raise new plants from seeds, or softwood cuttings in mid-summer.

## Cydonia oblonga

**Common Quince** (USA/UK)

Hardy, deciduous, thornless tree usually with crowded branches and a relatively low habit. The young branches are grayish and with oval or elliptic dark green leaves. During late spring it bears pink or white single flowers, later followed by light golden-yellow pear-shaped fruits.

It is ideal for many styles of bonsai, including informal upright, slanting, cascading and multiple trunks.

**Care:**
• Repot every other year during spring.
• Wait until the new shoots develop, then shorten them.
• Feed from late spring to late summer.
• Raise new plants from cuttings and by layering, as well as by sowing seeds.

## Daphne odora

**Winter Daphne** (USA)

Slightly tender, evergreen shrub with a bushy but lax nature and narrowly oval to oblong, shiny, mid-green leaves. It needs a sheltered position and protection from long, severe frosts. During mid- and late winter, and often into mid-spring, it bears terminal clusters of pale purple flowers that exude a sweet, spicy fragrance.

It is suitable for most styles of bonsai, including informal upright, slanting, both cascade and semi-cascade, and group.

**Care:**
• Repot every other year.
• Prune after the flowers fade by trimming back shoots. Take care not to prune before the display of flowers is over as the following season's display will be diminished.
• Feed from spring to late summer or early autumn.
• Raise plants from softwood cuttings.

## Daphne retusa

Evergreen shrub, often grown in rock gardens, with a rounded and bushy nature and somewhat pear-shaped, shiny, dark green, thickly textured leaves. In late spring and early summer it develops crowded, terminal clusters of rose-purple flowers. Their insides are paler and create a pleasing contrast. The flowers are fragrant, with a heavy and exotic perfume.

It is ideal for informal upright and slanting bonsai styles, as well as for semi-cascading.

**Care:**
- Repot every other year.
- Prune after the flowers fade by trimming back shoots. Take care not to prune before the display of flowers is over and the following season's display will be diminished.
- Feed from spring to late summer or early autumn.
- Raise new plants from seeds or softwood cuttings.

## Forsythia x intermedia

**Golden Bells** (USA)
Distinctive deciduous shrub which becomes emblazoned with dominant, bright color during spring. It has a stiff and compact nature and lance-shaped, tooth-edged, dark green leaves. During early and mid-spring it bears clusters of golden-yellow flowers; they appear on bare branches before the leaves arrive.

A smaller form is *Forsythia* x *intermedia* 'Minigold', which has a compact form and similar flowers.

It is ideal for many bonsai styles, including informal upright, slanting, both cascade and semi-cascade, and group.

**Care:**
- Repot every other year, during autumn.
- Prune after the flowers fade, severely cutting back shoots.
- Feed from spring through to early autumn.
- Raise new plants from hardwood cuttings in autumn.

## Fuchsia magellanica var. pumila

**Dwarf Hardy Fuchsia** (UK) **Lady's Eardrops** (USA/UK)
Hardy, deciduous shrub with lance-shaped, mid-green leaves in pairs on opposite sides of stems. Pendent, red and purple flowers are borne on short stems from mid-summer to autumn.

Several other fuchsias can be grown as bonsai, including *Fuchsia microphylla*, *Fuchsia* x *bacillaris*, *Fuchsia* 'Tom Thumb,' and *Fuchsia* 'Lady Thumb'.

Fuchsias can be grown in several bonsai styles, including informal upright, slanting, semi-cascade, and root-over-rock.

**Care:**
- Repot every year in spring.
- Prune throughout summer by pinching back new shoots to create a bushy plant.
- Feed from late spring to late summer or early autumn.
- Raise new plants from softwood cuttings in early summer.

## Hamamelis japonica

**Japanese Witch Hazel** (USA/UK)
Hardy, deciduous large shrub or small tree with a spreading nature and oval, glossy, mid-green leaves that, in autumn, assume rich shades of yellow and red. However, it is better known for its magnificent spider-like flowers that appear in late winter and early spring, before the leaves appear. The yellow flowers have twisted and crimped petals.

It is ideal for many bonsai styles, including informal upright, slanting, both cascade and semi-cascade, group, and root-over-rock.

**Care:**
- Repot every other year, in spring after the flowers fade.
- Prune new growth throughout summer.
- Feed from late spring to autumn.
- Raise new plants from cuttings.

## Jasminum nudiflorum

**Winter-flowering Jasmine** (UK) **Winter Jasmine** (USA)
Popular, deciduous, winter-flowering shrub, usually grown against a wall in temperate climates. The bright yellow, star-shaped flowers appear either singly or in small clusters from early winter to mid-spring on bare, flexible, arching, green stems.

It is suitable for several bonsai styles, including informal upright, slanting, semi-cascade, group, and root-over-rock.

**Care:**
- Repot every year, after the flowers fade or in autumn.
- Prune new shoots after the flowers fade, to one set of leaves. Additionally, in autumn, prune branches back to three or four sets of leaves.
- Feed from late spring to late summer.
- Raise new plants either from softwood cuttings in summer or from hardwood cuttings in autumn.

## *Laburnum alpinum*

**Golden-chain Tree** (USA/UK) **Golden Rain Tree** (UK) **Scotch Laburnum** (UK)
Beautiful, deciduous tree with a broad head and, increasingly with age, an old and gnarled appearance. This especially suits bonsai. The mid-green, glossy leaves create an attractive foil for the pendulous clusters of yellow flowers from late spring to early summer.

It is ideal for informal upright, slanting, cascade and semi-cascade, and group.
*Care:*
• Repot annually in spring.
• Prune after the flowers fade, trimming shoots to 2–3 buds.
• Feed from spring to autumn.
• Raise new plants from seeds.

## *Malus baccata*

**Siberian Crab** (USA/UK)
**Siberian Crab Apple** (USA/UK)
Deciduous tree with a rounded, wide-spreading head and arching or pendulous lower branches. The leaves are glossy green, oval and have shallowly toothed edges. In mid-spring, it bears clusters of white flowers, followed in autumn by bright red or yellow fruits.

It is ideal for several bonsai styles, including informal upright, slanting, and group.
*Care:*
• Repot every year in early spring, before the buds show color.
• Prune young, new shoots in spring, pinching them to 1–2 leaves. Additionally, in autumn trim back long shoots.
• Feed in spring, and again after the fruits are young and developing.
• Raise new plants from seeds in autumn.

## *Prunus 'Kanzan'*

**Japanese Flowering Cherry** (USA/UK)
Handsome, deciduous, widely branched tree with oval, taper-pointed, mid-green leaves that assume bronze-orange shading in autumn. They have bronze shades when young. In the latter half of mid-spring, it bears masses of double, light purple-pink flowers that can weigh down branches.

It is ideal for creating several styles of bonsai, except broom.
*Care:*
• Repot annually in spring, before the buds show color.
• Prune after the flowers fade. Throughout summer, pinch out the tips of young shoots.
• Feed from when the flowers fade to late summer.
• Raise new plants by grafts.

## *Spiraea japonica*

**Japanese Spiraea** (USA/UK)
Hardy, deciduous shrub with a twiggy nature and sharply tooth-edged, oval, mid-green leaves. During mid- and late summer it bears numerous flat heads of small pink flowers.

It can be grown in several styles, including informal upright, slanting, semi-cascade, cascade and group.
*Care:*
• Repot every other year, in spring.
• Prune back severely in spring. In late summer or early autumn, cut back long shoots.
• Feed from late spring to early autumn.
• Raise plants from softwood cuttings in early summer.

### Syringa meyeri var. spontanea 'Palibin'

Also known as *Syringa palibiniana*, this dwarf, slow-growing, deciduous shrub has a compact nature, with roundish to oval, dark green leaves, grayish-green beneath. In mid-spring, it develops lilac-pink, fragrant flowers.

Sometimes *Syringa vulgaris* (Common Lilac) is recommended, but this requires more pruning to restrict its growth.

It is ideal for several bonsai styles, including informal upright, slanting, both semi-cascade and cascade, group, and root-over-rock.

**Care:**
- Repot every other year, as soon as the flowers fade.
- Prune by trimming young shoots as soon as the flowers fade. Also trim long shoots in late summer.
- Feed from late spring to late summer.
- Raise new plants from softwood cuttings in summer.

### Tamarix ramosissima

**Tamarisk** (USA/UK)
Also known as *Tamarix pentandra*, this hardy deciduous shrub has awl-shaped, pale to mid-green leaves and, in late summer, produces masses of long, feathery flowerheads of rose-pink flowers. The whole plant has a willowy, slender appearance.

It can be grown in several bonsai styles, including informal upright, slanting, both cascade and semi-cascade, root-over-rock and clasped-to-rock.

**Care:**
- Repot annually or every other year, in early or mid-spring.
- Prune in late winter, cutting growth hard back. It will bear flowers on young growth.
- Feed from spring to late summer or into early autumn.
- Raise new plants from softwood cuttings in summer, or hardwood cuttings in early winter.

### Other Flowering Trees and Shrubs

- *Amelanchier lamarckii*
- *Andromeda polifolia*
- *Berberis darwinii*
- *Camellia japonica*
- *Camellia reticulata*
- *Camellia sasanqua*
- *Cercis siliquastrum*
- *Corylopsis pauciflora*
- *Corylopsis spicata*
- *Daphne burkwoodii*
- *Deutzia gracilis*
- *Escallonia* 'Apple Blossom'
- *Magnolia stellata*
- *Potentilla* spp.
- *Prunus serrulata*
- *Prunus subhirtella*
- *Weigela florida*

### Wisteria chinensis

**Chinese Wisteria** (USA/UK)
Vigorous, deciduous climber with mid- to dark green leaves, each formed of up to 11 leaflets. The beautiful mauve, fragrant flowers are borne in long, drooping clusters during late spring and early summer. There is also a white-flowered form.

It is ideal for bonsai styles such as informal upright, slanting, semi-cascade, cascade, and root-over-rock.

**Care:**
- Repot every 3–4 years, as soon as the flowers fade.
- Prune in spring, cutting back shoots to 2–3 leaves as soon as the flowers fade. Additionally, continue this pruning throughout summer and into early autumn.
- Feed from when the flowers fade to the latter part of mid-summer, then again in autumn.
- Raise new plants from hardwood cuttings in late autumn or early winter.

### Wisteria floribunda

**Japanese Wisteria** (USA/UK)
Well-known deciduous climber with slender branches and leaves, each formed of 12–19 oval leaflets. The spectacular, violet-blue, fragrant flowers are borne during late spring and early summer. There is also a white-flowered form.

It is ideal for bonsai styles such as informal upright, slanting, semi-cascade, cascade, and root-over-rock.

**Care:**
- Repot every 3–4 years, as soon as the flowers fade.
- Prune in spring, cutting back shoots to 2–3 leaves as soon as the flowers fade. Also, continue this pruning throughout summer and into early autumn.
- Feed from when the flowers fade to the latter part of mid-summer, then again in autumn.
- Raise new plants from hardwood cuttings in late autumn or early winter.

# ➔ A–Z of Fruiting Trees and Shrubs

The range of trees and shrubs that produce fruits and are suitable for bonsai is limited, but those that do certainly add a further facet to the art of bonsai and are especially welcome in autumn and winter. Many of these fruits are attractive to birds and may need protection. Unfortunately, birds not only eat the fruits but also damage buds and tear leaves.

Fruits epitomize autumn and perhaps none more so than *Malus* (Crab Apples). There are several species that create magnificent displays of round, small, apple-like fruits that ripen during autumn in colors ranging from yellow to red. Many, such as 'Yellow Siberian', persist well into winter.

The shrub-like Cotoneasters and Pyracanthas also create superb displays of fruits, while the evergreen shrub *Berberis darwinii* (Darwin's Berberis) reveals small, glossy, holly-like leaves and rich yellow spring flowers in addition to dark blue berries. *Berberis thunbergii* has pale yellow flowers and small, scarlet berries.

### Berries or Fruits?

Botanically, a fruit is a mature ovary together with ripe seeds. It may be soft and fleshy like a berry or dry like a nut. For autumn color, it is the soft and fleshy types that create interest.

---

### *Cotoneaster horizontalis*

**Fishbone Cotoneaster** (UK) **Herringbone Cotoneaster** (UK) **Rock Cotoneaster** (USA) **Rockspray Cotoneaster** (USA)

Distinctive, deciduous shrub with a low, flat nature (though it can be upright when against a wall) and branches that resemble a herringbone. These are clad in small, glossy, dark green leaves. Small, pink flowers appear in early summer, followed by small, round, red berries, which are especially conspicuous after leaves fall in autumn. It is ideal for bonsai styles such as informal upright, slanting, semi-cascade, cascade, group, root-over-rock, and clasp-to-rock.

*Care:*
- Repot annually when young, in early spring.
- Prune in early spring, cutting back long branches. During summer, trim back young shoots.
- Feed from early summer to early autumn.
- Raise new plants from softwood cuttings in summer, and hardwood cuttings in autumn or early winter.

### Other fruiting bonsai
- *Berberis buxifolia*
- *Berberis darwinii*
- *Berberis thunbergii*
- *Chaenomeles japonica*
- *Chaenomeles speciosa*
- *Chaenomeles x superba*
- *Cotoneaster adpressus*
- *Cotoneaster congestus*
- *Cotoneaster microphyllus*
- *Crataegus laevigata*
- *Crataegus monogyna*
- *Malus* 'Golden Hornet'
- *Malus* 'Profusion'
- *Prunus avium*
- *Pyracantha coccinea*

## Pyracantha angustifolia

**Firethorn** (USA/UK) **Narrow-leaf Firethorn** (USA)
Hardy, evergreen shrub with a spreading nature and narrow, oblong to oval, mid-green leaves. During early and mid-summer it bears cream-colored flowers, followed in autumn with bright orange-yellow berries.

It is ideal for informal upright, slanting, semi-cascade, cascade, group, and root-over-rock styles.

### Care:
- Repot every other year, in spring.
- Prune in late spring, trimming back new shoots to two leaves.
- Feed from spring to late summer.
- Raise new plants from seeds, and softwood cuttings in summer.

## Malus

**Crab Apple**
Hardy, deciduous trees with glossy, green, oval leaves. During spring, they bear clusters of bowl-shaped, slightly fragrant flowers in clusters at the ends of spurs. The round or slightly oval fruits, which resemble small apples, ripen in early autumn and into mid-autumn and range in color from yellow to red.

There are many superb trees to consider; *Malus baccata* is featured on page 63 and others are suggested below.

They are ideal for training in several bonsai styles, including informal upright, slanting, and group.

### Care:
- Repot annually in early spring, before the buds show color.
- Prune young, new shoots in spring, pinching them back to 1–2 leaves. Additionally, in autumn, trim back long shoots.
- Feed in spring, and again after the fruits are young and developing.
- Raise new plants by seeds in autumn.

# Indoor Bonsai

# Caring for Indoor Bonsai

### ◼ Can indoor bonsai be left indoors all year?

Unlike traditional outdoor bonsai (often known as Japanese bonsai), indoor bonsai (occasionally referred to as Chinese bonsai) is the selection of tropical and sub-tropical plants that can be treated in the same way as outdoor bonsai but, because of their tender nature, are kept indoors throughout the year in temperate climates. However, in warmer climates these plants would be candidates for growing outdoors.

## Sojourns or permanent homes?

There is often a misunderstanding about taking outdoor bonsai indoors. Bonsai books solely about outdoor bonsai (which are hardy plants) mention that they can be taken indoors, but this is for short periods and only if the temperature is not too high. They are not houseplants.

Indoor bonsai (which are tropical and sub-tropical plants) are not hardy outdoors in temperate climates and therefore spend their lives indoors in congenial warmth that is essential for their growth and well-being.

Heated conservatories and sun-rooms create homes for indoor bonsai, but unless they are heated day and night during winter the temperatures in them can fall rapidly, especially at night. Plants positioned near to the sides are the ones most likely to suffer from drops in temperature. Therefore, group them toward the center of the room.

### INEXPENSIVE INDOOR BONSAI

Indoor bonsai can be bought, but it is also possible to create your own—and inexpensively! Many houseplants can be converted into bonsai and these can be bought in garden centers and supermarkets. Plants to look for include those that are primarily grown for their attractive foliage, such as *Ficus benjamina* (Weeping Fig), *Ficus retusa* (Indian Laurel), *Nandina domestica* (Heavenly Bamboo) and *Punica granatum* (Pomegranate), as well as flowering types including Gardenias. Several other *Ficus* species can be used.

By pruning these plants—in much the same way as when creating an outdoor bonsai (see pages 30–31) from a shrub or tree bought from a garden center—indoor bonsai can be made.

*Varieties of* Ficus, *which are commonly grown as houseplants in cooler climates, make excellent indoor bonsai specimens.*

## Places in the House to Avoid

Growing bonsai indoors is exciting, but invariably it creates an artificial environment for them. Here are a few places to avoid.

- Corners where the light is poor and the plant's foliage is drawn to strong sunlight.
- Near to doors that are constantly being opened, causing cold draughts to blow on plants.
- Next to windows, where strong light might damage delicate and thin leaves.
- In a direct line from strong blasts of hot air.

## Going away on Holiday?

After enthusiastically caring for indoor bonsai throughout the year, the prospect of leaving them for a few weeks can be worrying. The best solution is to ask a fellow bonsai enthusiast to come in daily and to water them. Alternatively, place plants on a sheet of polythene on the floor in a cool, shaded room. This will help them to remain healthy for a few days.

## Can I put Indoor Bonsai Outdoors?

Yes, but only the toughest plants (such as some Ficus) and then just for short periods in a warm, sheltered position during summer. Avoid positions in cold, chilling draughts.

# INDOOR BONSAI GROWING GUIDE

When growing bonsai indoors, it is possible to use supplementary light to encourage growth and to keep plants healthy. However, do not use these lights continuously throughout a 24-hour cycle; instead, about 16 hours a day is best.

Use plant-friendly and growth-producing lights, such as fluorescent cool-white lights or 'grow' bulbs. Usually, it is only necessary to use supplementary light during winter or for longer periods in dark regions.

Engage a competent electrician to install the lights and ensure that all safety measures are introduced into the system. Water and electricity can be a lethal combination—never take risks where these are concerned.

## Temperature

In the wild there is a close relationship between temperature and the amount of light a plant receives. When plants are in an artificial environment, these often become out of balance.

- If the temperature is too high in relation to the available light, the plant will be too active and, eventually, become exhausted.
- If the temperature is too low in relation to the available light, the plant will not create growth.
- The temperature should be higher during the day than at night when the plant is relatively inactive.

## Light

Sunlight is the prime initiator of growth in plants, and although many tropical and sub-tropical types naturally live in diffused light, they do need good light when indoors and in temperate regions.

- Position plants in good light in winter, but slightly diffused in summer, especially if the leaves are thin and delicate.
- Rotate plants every 7–10 days if the main light is coming only from one position; if left in one place, shoots will be attracted to grow towards it and create a lop-sided and unattractive plant.

## Humidity

Mist-spraying the foliage of tropical and sub-tropical plants helps to keep them cool and better able to function when the temperature rises.

- Do not mist-spray flowers, as this soon causes them to decay. If spraying leaves is essential, place a small piece of card in front of the flowers.
- Mist-spray in the morning, so that all trace of moisture on leaves has disappeared by evening, when the temperature naturally falls.
- Standing a plant on pebbles in a shallow tray of water creates a humid atmosphere.

## Watering and Feeding

Regular watering is essential, especially throughout summer when the temperature rises dramatically. Remember—the larger the plant, the more water it requires. At each watering, thoroughly soak the compost and allow excess to drain.

- Water plants in the morning, so that by evening all excess moisture has evaporated.
- If the compost has become very dry, stand the pot about one-third deep in a bowl of water. Remove it when moisture reaches the surface and allow excess to drain.
- Do not let the compost become even slightly dry when the plant is bearing flowers, as this will limit the display.
- About every two weeks from mid-spring to early autumn, when plants are growing strongly, give them a weak liquid fertilizer when watered. At other times, feed them every 4–6 weeks. Do not feed when a plant is dormant.

## Repotting

Indoor bonsai are sometimes grown in slightly deeper pots than the shallow types used for outdoor plants, although this depends on the plant.

- Young indoor bonsai plants need repotting about every two years in spring. The pot is removed, roots loosened and cut back by about one-third. The plant is moved to a slightly larger pot, ½"–¾" (12–18mm) wider, and fresh compost added.
- With older and established plants, repot them when the roots fill the pot and are matted. Fewer roots will need to be removed and the bonsai can be replaced into a similar-sized pot. This may be needed every 4–5 years.

## Troubleshooting

Pests such as greenfly can be a problem both indoors and outdoors. When spraying plants indoors, take extra care and ensure that the spray is for indoor use and will not damage curtains and furniture. Additionally, always clear the room of children and pets (especially fish and birds) before using a spray. Do not spray near polished surfaces. Later, thoroughly ventilate the room. Sometimes the plant can be placed in a large plastic bag to be sprayed. Do not inhale the fumes. Always follow the manufacturer's instructions.

# A–Z of Indoor Bonsai

## ◼ What are indoor bonsai?

Indoor bonsai are tropical or sub-tropical woody plants, mainly those that have a wealth of small, green leaves. There are also several superb flowering plants that can be used for indoor bonsai. These include Bougainvilleas and Gardenias. Several tender succulents are also used, perhaps none more so than *Crassula arborescens*, a shrubby, tender plant in temperate climates and often grown in a greenhouse or as a houseplant. Many *Ficus* species are ideal as indoor bonsai.

## ➔ A–Z of Indoor Bonsai

These create interest throughout the year and in winter are a welcome respite from the gloom outdoors. Some foliage plants—such as *Ficus benjamina* (Weeping Fig)—which are used for indoor bonsai are relatively tough and often can be seen in reception areas of offices, where they survive strong light and cool draughts. Others are not so hardy and need warmth throughout the year.

The glorious *Hibiscus rosa-sinensis* (Rose of China) is less hardy. Earlier, in China, juice derived from the flowers was used to black shoes. *Nandina domestica* (Heavenly Bamboo) also has an interesting history in Japan; the aromatic wood was used as toothpicks, while it was planted in many courtyards and gardens and whenever someone in the household had a bad dream the problem was confided to the plant, which assured that it would not happen again.

The slow-growing *Cycas revoluta* (Sago Palm) is an unusual plant for bonsai and creates a distinctive feature—it is described and illustrated on the opposite page.

> ### Getting the Balance Right
> For indoor bonsai, choose a range of foliage and flowering plants so that interest is created throughout the year. Foliage plants are easier to grow in winter than flowering types, which are especially susceptible to cold draughts and hot blasts of air from heating systems.

### *Bouganvillea* x *buttiana*

**Bougainvillea** (USA/UK) **Paper-flower** (USA) A climber and popular hybrid of *Bougainvillea glabra* and *Bougainvillea peruviana*, with deep-red, flower-like bracts (a modified leaf that supplements or takes the place of a petal). These appear among oval, light green leaves.

There are several varieties, with bracts in colors including orange, deep red, cerise, and white.

In temperate climates, Bougainvilleas need to be closeted in the warmth of a greenhouse or house, but in warm countries, these glorious South American shrubby climbers create magnificent displays as outdoor climbers or as sprawling and colorful hedges and boundaries.

*Care:*
• Repot young plants every 3–4 years in spring.
• Prune in spring or summer, cutting back straggly shoots to create a neatly shaped plant.
• Feed as suggested on page 69.
• Raise new plants from cuttings in summer.

### *Carmona microphylla*

**Fukien Tea** (USA/UK) **Philippine Tea** (USA) Also known as *Carmona buxifolia*, *Ehretia buxifolia*, and *Ehretia microphylla*, this confusingly named plant is a tender, evergreen shrub. It displays small, dark green, glossy, oval leaves. In spring and early summer, it reveals white flowers, later followed by green berries that turn red.

*Care:*
• Repot young plants every two years in spring.
• Prune from spring to late summer by regularly trimming back new shoots to 2–3 leaves.
• Feed as suggested on page 69.
• Raise new plants from seeds as well as softwood cuttings taken in spring and summer.

## *Crassula arborescens*

**Chinese Jade Plant** (USA/UK) **Jade Plant** (USA/UK) **Jade Tree** (UK) **Silver Jade Plant** (USA) **Silver-dollar** (USA)

Also known as *Crassula cotyledon*, this distinctive succulent plant has rounded to pear-shaped, gray-green leaves that, together with the stems, retain large amounts of water. Sometimes, the leaves have red edges.

**Care:**
• Repot young plants every two years in spring; older plants when roots fill the pot.
• Prune in spring or early summer. After initially shaping the plant, each year wait until 2–3 pairs of new leaves have formed, then trim the shoot to one pair.
• Feed as suggested on page 69.
• Raise new plants from leaf cuttings in spring and summer.

## *Crassula ovata*

**Baby Jade Plant** (USA/UK) **Cauliflower Ears** (USA) **Chinese Rubber Plant** (USA) **Dollar Plant** (USA)

Also known as *Crassula argentea*, it forms a shrub outdoors in southern California, but in temperate climates, is better indoors. It develops flattened but succulent, pear-shaped, shiny green leaves with red edges. Eventually it creates a large and attractive trunk.

**Care:**
• Repot young plants every two years in spring; older plants when roots fill the pot.
• Prune in spring or early summer. After initially shaping the plant, each year wait until 2–3 pairs of new leaves have formed, then trim the shoot to one pair.
• Feed as suggested on page 69.
• Raise new plants from leaf cuttings in spring and summer.

## *Crassula sarcocaulis*

Dwarf and shrubby plant with woody stems and small, green, pointed leaves often flushed red, especially during summer. Additionally, from mid-summer to early autumn, it displays pink flowers, but with an unpleasant aroma. There is also an attractive and distinctive white-flowered form.

**Care:**
• Repot young plants every two years in spring; older plants when roots fill the pot. Add extra sharp sand to the potting mixture.
• Prune in spring or early summer. After initially shaping the plant, pinch back young shoots. Additionally, remove leaves from the trunk.
• Feed as suggested on page 69.
• Raise new plants from cuttings in spring and summer.

## *Cycas revoluta*

**Japanese Fern Palm** (USA) **Japanese Sago Palm** (USA) **Sago Palm** (USA/UK)

A primitive plant with a palm-like appearance. However, it is not a true palm. It is a tender plant and has a slow-growing nature, often adding just one new leaf a year. The leaves form a beautiful rosette of stiff and arching foliage.

**Care:**
• Repot young plants every two years in spring.
• Pruning is not necessary—indeed, it would spoil the distinctive shape of the plant.
• Feed as suggested on page 69, but not during winter. Always use a weak fertilizer solution.
• Raise new plants by division.

## Ficus benjamina

**Benjamin Tree** (USA) **Java Fig** (USA) **Small-leaved Rubber Plant** (USA) **Weeping Fig** (USA/UK) **Weeping Laurel** (USA)

Graceful, weeping tree with woody stems and slender, pendulous side branches that bear soft green leaves that, with age, slowly become darker.

There are attractive forms, some with variegated leaves, others narrow.

### Care:
- Repot young plants every two years in spring; older plants when roots fill the pot.
- Prune in spring or early summer. Cut off unwanted branches and allow light and air to enter. Remove upward-growing stems. White fluid will run out of the cut stems; use a wound sealant. During late spring and summer, pinch back young shoots to 2–3 leaves.
- Feed as suggested on page 69.
- Raise new plants from cuttings.

## Ficus barteri

**South African Veldt Fig** (UK)

This distinctive Fig from western and tropical Africa creates a shrub or small tree with somewhat elliptical and pointed mid- to bright green leaves. The undersides are paler but nevertheless attractive. In the wild, it develops orange or orange-yellow figs, either solitarily or in pairs.

### Care:
- Repot young plants every two years in spring; older plants when roots fill the pot.
- Prune in spring or early summer to reduce the plant's size and to encourage light and air to enter the plant.
- Feed as suggested on page 69.
- Raise new plants from cuttings in summer.

## Ficus macrophylla

**Australian Banyan** (USA) **Moreton Bay Fig** (USA/UK)

A distinctive tree with an attractive and bulbous base to its trunk. In addition, it develops aerial roots. In the wild, it creates a large tree, but in a container, its glossy, leathery leaves are much smaller.

### Care:
- Repot young plants every two years in spring; older plants when roots fill the pot.
- Prune in spring or early summer. Cut off unwanted branches and allow light and air to enter. Remove upward-growing stems. White fluid will run out of the cut stems; use a wound sealant. During late spring and summer, pinch back young shoots to two leaves.
- Feed as suggested on page 69.
- Raise new plants from cuttings in summer.

## Ficus microcarpa

**Banyan fig** (UK) **Chinese Banyan** (USA) **Glossy-leaf Fig** (USA) **Indian Laurel** (USA/UK) **Malay Banyan** (USA)

Also known as *Ficus retusa*, this distinctive shrub or tree has broadly oval, glossy-green leaves that thickly clothe the branches. It also develops aerial roots, which introduce a further focus of interest.

### Care:
- Repot young plants every two years in spring; older plants when roots fill the pot.
- Prune in spring or early summer. Cut off unwanted branches and allow light and air to enter. Remove upward-growing stems. White fluid will run out of the cut stems; use a wound sealant. During late spring and summer, pinch back young shoots to two leaves.
- Feed as suggested on page 69.
- Raise new plants from cuttings in summer.

## Ficus rubiginosa

**Little-leaf Fig** (USA) **Port Jackson Fig** (USA) **Rusty Fig** (USA) **Rusty-leaved Fig** (USA/UK)
Attractive, small tree, with leathery, oval to elliptic, glossy, dark green leaves often covered with a rust-colored down. There is a beautiful form with creamy-yellow leaves.

**Care:**
- Repot young plants every two years in spring; older plants when roots fill the pot.
- Prune in spring or early summer. Cut off unwanted branches and allow light and air to enter. Also, cut out upward-growing stems. White fluid will run out of the cut stems; use a wound sealant. Throughout summer, pinch back young shoots to create an attractive shape full of young shoots and leaves.
- Feed as suggested on page 69.
- Raise new plants from softwood cuttings in summer.

## Fortunella hindsii

**Dwarf Kumquat** (USA/UK) **Dwarf Orange** (UK) **Hong Kong Kumquat** (USA) **Hong Kong Wild Kumquat** (USA)
Distinctive, tender, evergreen shrub with oval, glossy, deep green leaves and small, fragrant white flowers. Sometimes it develops fruits that ripen to bright tangerine-orange to flame-orange. However, unless temperature and humidity are high, the possibility of producing attractive fruits is unlikely.

**Care:**
- Repot young plants every 2–3 years in spring.
- Prune throughout summer, trimming back young shoots.
- Feed as suggested on page 69.
- Raise new plants from seeds and softwood cuttings.

## Gardenia jasminoides

**Cape Jasmine** (USA/UK) **Common Gardenia** (USA) **Gardenia** (UK)
Tender, evergreen shrub famed for its strongly fragrant flowers, especially the double forms. In earlier years, they were extensively used to decorate and bring fragrance to dining tables, as well as to buttonholes. The leaves are glossy-green and lance-shaped, and borne in whorls of three. The flowers are borne from leaf-axils and flowering is from early to late summer.

**Care:**
- Repot young plants every two years in spring; use lime-free potting compost.
- Prune after the flowers fade, trimming back new shoots to maintain the shrub's shape.
- Feed as suggested on page 69.
- Raise new plants from softwood cuttings in summer.

## Hibiscus rosa-sinensis

**Blacking Plant** (USA) **China Rose** (USA) **Chinese Hibiscus** (USA) **Hawaiian Hibiscus** (USA) **Rose of China** (USA/UK)
Spectacular tender climber with broadly oval, dark green, tooth-edged and pointed leaves. It flowers over a long period, from early summer to early autumn, with single, deep crimson flowers.

**Care:**
- Repot young plants every two years in spring.
- Prune in spring, trimming back new shoots to maintain the shrub's shape.
- Feed as suggested on page 69.
- Raise new plants from softwood cuttings in summer.

## Jacaranda mimosifolia

**Green Ebony** (USA) **Jacaranda** (UK)
Also known as *Jacaranda ovalifolia* and *Jacaranda acutifolia*, this elegant, deciduous tree has mid- to light green, fern-like leaves borne on long, slightly cascading stems. Indoors, it seldom develops its violet flowers.

**Care:**
- Repot young plants every two years in spring. Use lime-free compost.
- Prune with great care, as the plant's attractiveness could be ruined. All that is required is to pinch out young shoots to create an attractive shape.
- Feed as suggested on page 69.
- Raise new plants from seeds.

## Ligustrum sinensis

**Chinese Privet** (USA/UK)
Hardy deciduous shrub—
or in mild winters nearly
evergreen—with a dense
habit packed with pale green,
oval, or elliptic leaves. As
well as being grown indoors,
where it retains its foliage (but
ensure the temperature is not
excessively high), it can be
grown as an outdoor bonsai.
However, when outdoors it
may lose its leaves during cold
winters.

### Care:
• Repot young plants every
  other year; with age, leave
  this until the container is full
  of roots.
• Prune throughout summer—it has a rapid growing nature and the shoots tend to
  expand quickly.
• Feed as suggested on page 69.
• Raise new plants from cuttings during summer.

## Luma apiculata

**Arrayan** (USA) **Collimamol** (USA)
**Palo Colorado** (USA)
Also known as *Myrtus apiculata*, this
evergreen, slightly tender shrub or small
tree has cinnamon-colored bark, which
peels to an ash-gray shade underneath.
The oval leaves are dull green, with small,
white flowers during summer. The flowers
are followed by black and red fruits.

### Care:
• Repot young plants every two years in
  spring.
• Prune throughout summer, pinching
  back young shoots to create an attractive
  shape and to restrict the plant's size.
• Feed as suggested on page 69.
• Raise new plants from cuttings during
  summer.

## Murraya paniculata

**Chinese Box** (USA)
**Cosmetic Bark
Tree** (USA) **Orange
Jasmine** (USA/UK)
**Orange Jessamine**
(USA/UK)
**Satinwood** (USA)
**Satinwood Tree**
(UK)
Tropical, evergreen
shrub or small tree
with dainty, small,
mid- to dark green,
somewhat pear-
shaped, pleasantly
aromatic leaves. It

is best known for its fragrant, white, bell-shaped flowers which
drench the air with a jasmine-like bouquet. The flowers are
followed by small, orange-like fruits.

### Care:
• Repot young plants every two years in spring.
• Prune throughout summer, pinching back young shoots to
  create an attractive shape and to restrict the plant's size.
• Feed as suggested on page 69.
• Raise new plants from seeds and softwood cuttings.

## Myrtus communis

**Common Myrtle** (UK) **Greek Myrtle** (USA)
**Indian Buchu** (USA) **Myrtle** (USA/UK)
**Swedish Myrtle** (USA)
Tender, evergreen shrub with glossy,
mid- to dark green, oval to lance-
shaped aromatic leaves. It produces
white, fragrant flowers from
early to late summer, sometimes
followed by purple-black fruits. In
earlier times, the fragrant flowers
were used to create the toilet
water *eau d'ange*. The flowers are
sometimes used in salads.

### Care:
• Repot young plants every two years, in
  spring.
• Prune throughout summer, pinching
  back young shoots to create an attractive
  shape and to restrict the plant's size.
• Feed as suggested on page 69.
• Raise new plants from cuttings during
  summer.

## Nandina domestica

**Chinese Sacred Bamboo** (UK) **Heavenly Bamboo** (USA/UK) **Sacred Bamboo** (USA/UK)

Slightly tender, evergreen shrub with long, narrow, pale to mid-green leaves when mature. When young, they are stained and shaded red; in autumn, they assume shades of purple. Sometimes, plants develop white flowers in wide clusters during mid-summer, followed by scarlet or white fruits.

*Care:*
• Repot young plants every two years in spring.
• Prune throughout summer, pinching back young shoots to create an attractive shape and to restrict the plant's size.
• Feed as suggested on page 69.
• Raise plants from seeds and cuttings.

## Olea europaea

**Common Olive** (USA/UK) **Edible Olive** (USA)

Widely grown, slightly tender tree or shrub with oval to lance-shaped, shiny, dark green leaves with light gray undersides. The bark is attractive, light gray and becomes increasingly gnarled. The cream flowers are insignificant and, later, it produces the well-known green fruits, which ripen to black.

*Care:*
• Repot young plants every two years in spring.
• Prune throughout summer by pinching back young shoots to create bushiness and to maintain the small size of the plant.
• Feed as suggested on page 69.
• Raise plants from seeds and cuttings.

## Pistacia vera

**Fustuq** (USA) **Green Almond** (USA) **Pistachio** (UK) **Pistachio Nut** (USA) **Pistachio Nut Tree** (USA/UK)

Small, tender, spreading, deciduous tree with shiny green, oval to lance-shaped leaves with dull green undersides. Brownish-green flowers appear in late spring, followed by long, oval, reddish fruits.

*Care:*
• Repot young plants every two years in early summer, after the flowers fade.
• Prune throughout summer by pinching back young shoots to create bushiness and to maintain the small size of the plant.
• Feed as suggested on page 69.
• Raise plants from seeds and cuttings.

## Punica granatum

**Pomegranate** (USA/UK)

Tender, warmth-loving, branching, deciduous shrub or small tree with glossy, bright green, oval to oblong leaves borne on reddish stalks. It requires high temperatures for plants to produce the round, edible, yellow-flushed red fruits. However, the foliage is very attractive.

*Punica granatum* var. *nana* is smaller and often grown as a houseplant, when it occasionally produces both red, tubular flowers and bright orange fruits.

### Care:
- Repot young plants every two years in early spring. Later, repot when roots fill the pot.
- Prune throughout summer by pinching back young shoots to create bushiness and to maintain the small size of the plant.
- Feed as suggested on page 69.
- Raise new plants from seeds, or from softwood cuttings during summer.

## Sageretia thea

Also known as *Sageretia theezans*, this evergreen shrub creates an attractive indoor bonsai, with a trunk that reveals peeling and patterned bark. The branches are slender and bear small, oval, shiny, dark green leaves. It also reveals small, fragrant, white flowers and, later, purplish-black berries.

### Care:
- Repot young plants every two years in spring.
- Prune throughout summer by pinching back young shoots to 1–2 pairs of leaves. This will help to keep the plant small and neat.
- Feed as suggested on page 69.
- Raise new plants from softwood cuttings in spring or summer.

## Schefflera actinophylla

**Australian Ivy Palm** (USA) **Australian Umbrella Tree** (USA) **Octopus Tree** (USA) **Queensland Umbrella Tree** (USA) **Starleaf** (USA) **Umbrella Tree** (UK)

Also known as *Brassaia actinophylla*, this tender, evergreen tree develops leaves each formed of an umbrella-like arrangement of bright green, shiny, oblong to oval leaflets with long stalks. Mature plants usually have leaves formed of five leaflets; young plants only three. Additionally, the trunk sometimes produces aerial roots.

### Care:
- Repot young plants every two years in spring.
- Prune in spring or early summer; cut shoots hard back in order to encourage branching.
- Feed as suggested on page 69.
- Raise new plants from cuttings.

## Schefflera elegantissima

**False Aralia** (USA/UK) **Finger Aralia** (USA/UK)
Also known as *Aralia elegantissima* and *Dizygotheca elegantissima*, this distinctive and popular plant has long, saw-edged, dark green leaflets; when young they are coppery-red. The leaves are formed of 7–10 of these leaflets, attached to stiff, upright, woody stems.

*Care:*
- Repot young plants every two years in spring; older plants when roots fill the pot.
- Prune in spring or early summer. Cut off leaves from low down on the stems, but do not prune the individual leaves as the result will not be attractive.
- Feed as suggested on page 69.
- Raise new plants from seeds sown in late winter and early spring.

## Serissa foetida

**Tree of a Thousand Stars** (UK)
Also known as *Serissa japonica*, this distinctive, tender, evergreen shrub has smooth, dark green, oval to lance-shaped leaves. The white flowers are usually single, but double-flowered ones are known. Additionally, some forms have variegated leaves. It is the unpleasant odor emitted by the roots and bark that give rise to the *foetida* part of its name.

*Care:*
- Repot every two years in spring.
- Prune in spring or early summer, trimming young shoots to create a neat outline and to maintain a small plant.
- Feed as suggested on page 69.
- Raise new plants from softwood cuttings in early summer.

## Inexpensive Indoor Bonsai from Seeds

Many plants for indoor bonsai can be bought from garden centers, but a cheaper way is to raise your own from seeds of oranges and lemons. It is an exciting and often experimental way to raise your own plants and one that always results in questions from visitors.

- *Citrus limon* (Lemon) has elliptic, dark green leaves and fragrant, red-flushed white flowers during late spring and early summer. The small fruits take about a year to ripen.
- *Citrus mitis* (properly known as *Citrofortunella microcarpa* and widely known as Calamondin, Calamondin Orange and Panama Orange) is popular and small, with 1"–1½" (25–36mm) wide fruits even on small plants.
- *Citrus sinensis* (Sweet Orange) has larger fruits and in warm conservatories and greenhouses forms bushes about 4' (1.2m) high; as a bonsai it is less.

*Sow one seed in each pot, pressing it about ½" (12mm) deep.*

**Raising new plants:** Sow seeds in pots of well-drained seed compost in early or mid-spring and place them in 61°F (16°C). Keep the compost moist, but not saturated, and when the seedlings are large enough to handle transfer them into small, individual pots.

Reduce the temperature slightly and grow them until plants are large enough to be pruned and trained as bonsai.

## Other Indoor Bonsai to Consider

- *Acacia* (Wattle)
- *Allamanda cathartica* (Golden Trumpet)
- *Grevillea* (Silk Oak)
- *Ixora* (Flame of the Woods)
- *Ulmus parvifolia* (Chinese Elm)

**Ulmus parvifolia**

# Special Displays

# Displaying Outdoor Bonsai

## ◼ How do I display my bonsai?

Bonsai are best seen at or just below eye height, although for practical reasons, this is not always possible. Permanent staging, perhaps attached to a wall, is one way of displaying plants, but it should not be in continual shade. Other ways are on free-standing staging, on "monkey poles" (small platforms at the tops of stout wooden or concrete supports), or on tall display stands where cascading bonsai can be placed.

## Changing Positions

Where trees are displayed on staging positioned against a wall and perhaps in poor sunlight, regularly rotate each plant so that all parts receive equal amounts of light. Avoid positions in cold, strong draughts, as this may damage the foliage. Conversely, remember that displays close to walls may become excessively hot in summer when strong sunlight is reflected by a white or light-colored wall.

## Making Plants Comfortable

Where strong wind is a persistent problem, vertically slatted screening (with small spaces between strips of wood) helps to reduce the wind's speed without causing strong eddies on the lee side, as often produced by solid walls. Small areas can be made more hospitable by a bamboo screen, which also introduces a color and texture that is ideal for displaying bonsai. Backgrounds should not dominate the plants.

An overhead, sloping, slatted canopy formed of pieces of dark brown wood helps to limit the amount of direct sunlight plants receive. Paint it with a plant-friendly preservative and leave for several weeks to weather before positioning plants underneath the overhead screen.

### Display Notes
**Here are a few clues to success when displaying bonsai outdoors.**

- Avoid positioning bonsai in a place where you have to look down on them. Part of the pleasure of some bonsai is to see between the layers of branches.
- Where a bonsai container is positioned in a shallow water-basin, ensure that moisture is not able to seep into the compost, keeping it constantly wet. In such circumstances, the roots will eventually decay and die.
- If the size of the display area allows, position dwarf and slow-growing conifers in tubs on the paved or shingled surface. Bamboos can be planted directly into the soil or in wooden containers, or grown as bonsai (see pages 92–93).
- Where cascading bonsai are displayed, ensure that the stem and foliage are able to trail freely and the container is secure. Additionally, check that wind gusting around the cascading stems cannot cause plants to be blown about and damaged. The deep containers used for cascading bonsai help to give plants stability; nevertheless, they are easily toppled by inquisitive cats and gusting wind.

*Displaying outdoor bonsai where they can be readily admired is an essential part of bonsai gardening. Here, they are displayed on firm, raised, concrete surfaces.*

# OUTDOOR DISPLAY OPTIONS

Growing plants to perfection and then displaying them is all part of the art of bonsai. There are several ways to display outdoor bonsai and some of these are described and illustrated here. Always display them securely.

Using shingle as a flooring for the display area—with flagstones positioned as stepping areas—both creates a natural arena and acts as a deterrent to slugs and snails. If the sub-soil is well drained, rain rapidly drains through the shingle, enabling dry and easy access to plants.

## "Monkey Poles"

"Monkey poles" are vertical supports with small platforms at their tops, on which bonsai can be displayed. They are at various heights and therefore enable plants of differing sizes to be displayed at eye height. They are also useful for filling vertical space to obstruct unsightly features low down and in the background. Prostrate conifers are ideal for planting between them. Because plants are exposed on all sides to the elements, there is a risk of strong, gusting wind dislodging them.

## Free-Standing Staging

Free-standing staging is versatile and can, if desired, be moved to another position. Additionally, free-standing staging can be placed where plants are in good light. Wide staging enables better displays than narrow ones.

## Slatted Staging

Slatted staging positioned against a wall is often used to display bonsai, but ensure it is not constantly in shade. Slatted staging encourages a continuous circulation of air around plants and containers, helping to prevent the onset of diseases. Additionally, in summer, the circulation of air prevents compost in containers becoming excessively hot.

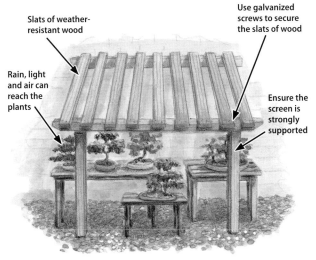

Slats of weather-resistant wood

Use galvanized screws to secure the slats of wood

Rain, light and air can reach the plants

Ensure the screen is strongly supported

## Shallow Water Basins

Shallow water basins create eye-catching features. In spring, light green shoots appear at the ends of shoots and look attractive when reflected in the water, especially when in bright sunlight.

Avoid creating large areas of water, as instead of being an unusual feature, it can be overwhelming. It also makes access to individual plants slightly difficult. Unfortunately, the water often attracts birds that might also be tempted to eat buds.

# Forest Bonsai from a Single Tree

## How do I create a forest display?

A forest display can be created by potting a group of individual plants in a container, but a more interesting way is from a single tree. This method produces a group of trees with the same characteristics, and not a diverse group of species in which some will be more vigorous than others and eventually dominate the display. Both deciduous and evergreen species can be used to create a forest display. Evergreen species create interest throughout the year.

## Creating a Deciduous Forest

Acers (Japanese Maples), *Carpinus betulus* (Hornbeam) and *Zelkova serrata* (Japanese Zelkova or Saw-leaf Zelkova) are suitable for producing a deciduous forest. Spring is the best time to start, so choose a garden-center tree in a pot with several low branches.

Prepare a container (see opposite) and cut each branch back to one bud. Remove the pot and lay the pruned tree on the compost; check that none are near the container's edges. Cut off coarse roots and those growing upward.

Secure the trunk and roots in the same way used for the evergreen conifer on the opposite page, and cover and firm compost over them. Add a thin layer of pea-shingle over the surface, and gently but thoroughly water the compost.

Shoots will grow from the buds on the pruned branches; retain the best and cut off the rest. Later, pinch out young shoots several times to encourage the development of further new shoots to fill out the display.

← Forest bonsai create a dominant and eye-catching display. Here is a distinctive display created from a pine, forming an attractive group.

→ As well as being created from a single tree, forests can be formed from a number of individual seed-raised plants grown together.

## Forest Variations

Forests vary, and this fact can be reflected in the nature of the display. Some forests are dense; others are swept by coastal winds. A few reveal an open area, especially when free of leaves.

Straight trunks of these Spruces create an impression of a deep, dense forest. Create a variation in height.

For coastal depictions, create a windswept scene where some trees are small and stunted by the continuous wind.

A few trees, near to the edge of a container and forming a small grove, create a feeling of vast space.

## Aftercare

**For the evergreen conifer …**
- As soon as the branches have assumed a permanent, upright nature, carefully remove the wires.
- Keep the compost moist and undisturbed for several months.

**For the deciduous tree …**
- By repeatedly pinching back shoots, a forest of young shoots is created.
- Keep the compost moist.
- Regularly check the tree for greenfly infestations—they like the soft, young shoots that appear in spring.

# HOW TO MAKE A FOREST BONSAI FROM A SINGLE TREE

Forest displays always attract attention and invariably an explanation is demanded by visitors about the way it was achieved. This forest is formed of an evergreen conifer and therefore provides interest throughout the year. The forest created on the opposite page is formed of deciduous trees and these have the benefit of beautiful autumnal color. Forest displays create a more relaxed and informal feature than upright forms of a single plant. Therefore, when in a collection of bonsai, they are useful for creating changes of style and form.

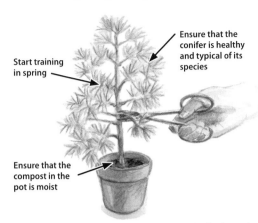

Ensure that the conifer is healthy and typical of its species

Start training in spring

Ensure that the compost in the pot is moist

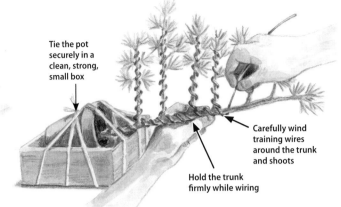

Tie the pot securely in a clean, strong, small box

Carefully wind training wires around the trunk and shoots

Hold the trunk firmly while wiring

**1** Early spring—when growth is beginning—is the best time to start training an evergreen conifer to form a forest. Select a young conifer and cut away unwanted branches close to the trunk. Leave an odd number of branches on the tree.

**2** To enable the pruned tree to be wired, temporarily tie the pot in a relatively small box so that it is held firm and there is no risk of movement. Wire the trunk to create undulations, with all of the branches held vertically by other pieces of wire. Some of the branches can be wired easily, but others may need greater manipulation.

Use wire to tie the plant into position

Use a container that does not constrict the display

Ensure the container is deep enough to accommodate the roots

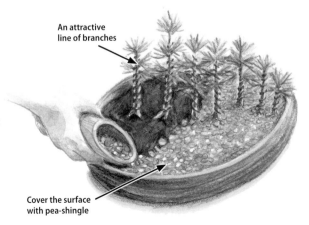

An attractive line of branches

Cover the surface with pea-shingle

**3** Prepare a container that is wide and long enough to accommodate the display. Place plastic mesh over the drainage holes and secure them with loop-ended wires (see page 23). Thread securing wires through the holes and spread a layer of flint chippings over the base, then a layer of potting compost. Remove the plant from its pot and position it in the container; reduce the size of the rootball, cutting away large, coarse roots. Tie the plant into position. If necessary, use pieces of soft leather to protect the trunk from the wires.

**4** Firm compost around the trunk and add a thin layer of pea-shingle over the surface. Thoroughly water the compost from above by using a fine-rosed watering-can. Allow excess water to drain and place in good light, but out of strong sunlight. Leave the plants undisturbed for several months, until they are established. Later, the wires can be removed.

# Bonsai on a Rock

## ■ How difficult is this bonsai?

It may take several years to create a perfect bonsai growing on or over a rock, but it is worth doing. There are two forms. The *root-over-rock* style involves training a plant's roots to grow over a rock, which is positioned on compost in a container. The *root-on-rock* style is where roots are growing in a pocket (or pockets) of humus (decayed plant debris) in clefts and holes in the rock.

## Root-On-Rock Style

Sometimes known as clasped-to-rock or stone-clasping bonsai, this style uses a rock to represent a mountain with a tree growing on it. Suitable rocks are hard and will not crumble; avoid quartz, marble, and sandstone. Tufa is ideal, and creating a tufa-bonsai feature is described on the right.

Because the tree is entirely on the rock, anchorage wires are glued (epoxy resin or a proprietary bonsai adhesive) to rocks for later holding plants in place. Roots and selected crevices are coated in a moist mixture of equal parts peat and clay, and wires are used to secure them. Use several small plants, not just one large tree.

When complete, position the rock in a shallow container, with fine gravel surrounding it. Add water to the container to highlight the feature.

*In the wild, roots of trees, often in old country lanes and woodland, are exposed.*

*This well-established root-over-rock bonsai creates an eye-catching feature and one that will fascinate your friends.*

### Bonsai on Tufa

Tufa is a porous limestone rock that absorbs and retains moisture. As well as being used as a base for a bonsai feature, tufa is used in scree beds and for growing alpine plants. Hollows can be chiseled out of it to accommodate roots. Do not use lime-hating plants, such as Azaleas, for tufa bonsai, as they need slightly acidic compost.

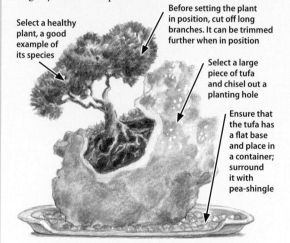

Select a healthy plant, a good example of its species

Before setting the plant in position, cut off long branches. It can be trimmed further when in position

Select a large piece of tufa and chisel out a planting hole

Ensure that the tufa has a flat base and place in a container; surround it with pea-shingle

**Step 1:** Select a piece of clean tufa and chisel out a planting hole in the "face side" of the display. Soak the tufa in a bucket of water for a day or so. Then remove it and allow to drain.

**Step 2:** Select a small, evergreen conifer and rake some of the soil from its roots. Do not remove more soil than is necessary. Cut back old, long, and thick roots.

**Step 3:** Place the roots of the tree in the hole and work potting compost around them. The tree should be held firmly at a natural and attractive angle.

**Step 4:** Use sharp scissors to trim the tree's foliage, so that it harmonizes with the tufa. Then, gently but thoroughly, water the compost. Take care that the compost does not become washed out, especially before the roots hold the plant in place.

# CREATING A ROOT-OVER-ROCK BONSAI

Keep in mind when creating a root-over-rock bonsai that, when finished, it must appear to be a tree growing naturally over a rock, not just perched precariously on top. A plant is pruned and positioned on top; the upper roots are exposed, but subsequently the lower ones grow into the compost to secure the plant and to gain moisture and nutrients. The container holds compost and the rock is placed on top and held in place with string or wires.

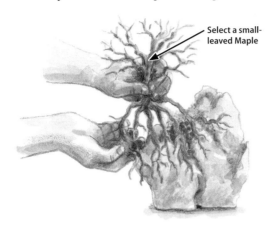

Select a small-leaved Maple

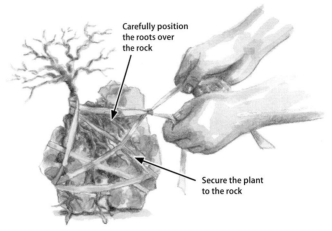

Carefully position the roots over the rock

Secure the plant to the rock

**1** In early spring, just before buds break open, choose a small, non-bonsai tree from a garden center. Small-leaved Maples are ideal, or a low-growing Juniper if an evergreen conifer is preferred. Here, a deciduous tree is shown. Select a weathered rock with a saddle-like depression at its top.

**2** Cut away some of the upper growth to create a balanced shape. Then use a small rake to pull away compost from the roots to expose them. Place a mixture of peat and clay over the rock, divide the roots into four bunches and position them over it. Use string, raffia, or wire (which lasts longer) to secure roots to the rock.

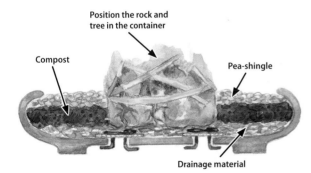

Compost

Position the rock and tree in the container

Pea-shingle

Drainage material

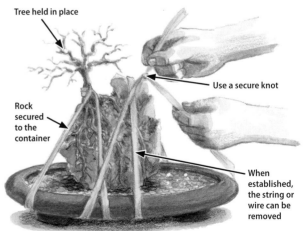

Tree held in place

Rock secured to the container

Use a secure knot

When established, the string or wire can be removed

**3** Prepare the container (see page 23), by placing plastic mesh over the drainage hole. Partly bury the rock's base. Bury as many roots as possible in the compost. Draw up compost around the roots and rock. This will help them to remain pliable and, eventually, to secure the plant.

**4** To keep the compost and upper roots moist, cover them with moist sphagnum moss. If the rock is not secure, use string or wire around the rock and container to hold them in place. Later, these can be removed. Frequently spray the roots and sphagnum moss with clean water to keep them moist.

# Group Bonsai

## ▪ Are groups difficult to create?

Skill is required to produce a natural-looking group formed of individual trees (creating a forest from a single tree is described on page 85). Usually, five or seven individual trees are needed, depending on the size of the container—always use an odd number, as this creates an informal and relaxed display. Group bonsai is created from deciduous trees, as well as evergreen or deciduous conifers. Deciduous trees create superb displays in spring, as well as in autumn.

## Planning Group Bonsai

It is essential that groups of bonsai mimic clusters of trees growing naturally. When selecting a suitable tree for group bonsai, remember these points.

- Because containers are relatively shallow, select those species that do not mind radical root reduction.
- Small-leaved (and needle-leaved) trees create a better display in a small container than those with large leaves.
- For added contrast, choose species with young leaves that differ in color from older foliage. This has the advantgae of creating both shape and color contrast.
- By preference, select plants of the same species. Some bonsai authorities even suggest raising your own plants from the same parent to ensure they are similar.

## With Maturity

As group bonsai age, they assume greater fascination, often more so than an aged and dignified tree on its own in a container. Pruning will be needed to keep the trees healthy and producing new growth. Because there are several trees in the display, if one is damaged or growth weakens, it is possible to train branches to fill gaps to maintain the display.

### Group Shapes to Avoid

Although there is flexibility in group design, and experimentation is to be encouraged, a group of bonsai must look natural and with a focal point. Avoid having tall trees at each end and lower ones in the center, as this will confuse the eye.

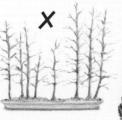

← Taller trees at the ends are visually confusing

➜ A focal point is created by placing tall trees in the center

## SUITABLE SPECIES FOR GROUP BONSAI

**Many different species can be used, including:**
**Deciduous trees:** *Fagus* (Beech), *Ulmus* (Elm), *Carpinus* (Hornbeam), *Acer* (Japanese Maple), *Zelkova*
**Deciduous conifers:** *Larix* (Larch)
**Evergreen conifers:** *Juniperus* (Juniper), *Cryptomeria*, *Cedrus* (Cedar), *Picea* (Spruce), *Pinus* (Pine)

← In nature, groups of trees dot the landscape and create focal points, as well as bringing interest to flat or slightly undulating areas.

➜ Group bonsai are dominant and when positioned among other specimens of bonsai help to bring variation and contrast.

## Other Designs

As well as the traditional, gently sloping design formed from a continuous and near-even planting of trees, other designs are possible and include one where there are three distinct groups. The top of the central group should be slightly above that of its neighbors.

# HOW TO PLANT A BONSAI GROUP

When selecting trees to form a group in the same container, choose those of same species. In nature, woodland groups are often formed of different species, but if mixed when in a cluster in a small container, the stronger trees will soon dominate the others.

Apart from deciduous trees, deciduous conifers such as *Larix kaempferi* (also known as *Larix leptolepis*; Japanese Larch) and evergreen conifers are used. Deciduous trees are especially attractive in spring when arrayed with young, fresh leaves, as well as in autumn when a few assume rich tints. Deciduous conifers are attractive in spring when fresh foliage appears.

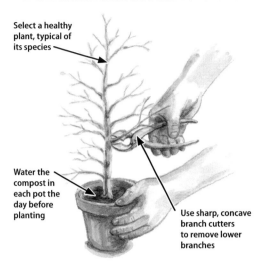

Select a healthy plant, typical of its species

Water the compost in each pot the day before planting

Use sharp, concave branch cutters to remove lower branches

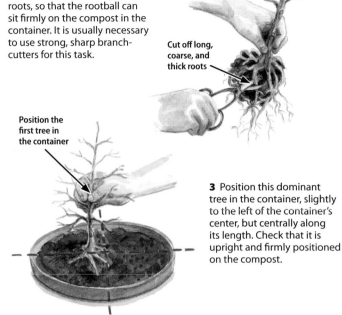

**2** Cut away any long, coarse roots, so that the rootball can sit firmly on the compost in the container. It is usually necessary to use strong, sharp branch-cutters for this task.

Cut off long, coarse, and thick roots

Position the first tree in the container

**3** Position this dominant tree in the container, slightly to the left of the container's center, but centrally along its length. Check that it is upright and firmly positioned on the compost.

**1** Select seven young trees, in pots and from a garden center (or raise your own). Prepare the container (see page 23). Choose the tallest and most dominant tree and use strong, concave branch cutters to cut away the lower branches, so that the lowest one is about one-third of the tree's height above the compost.

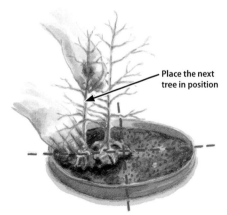

Place the next tree in position

**4** Select the second-largest tree in your group and position it to the left of the first tree. Then, choose the third-largest tree and position it to the right of the first tree.

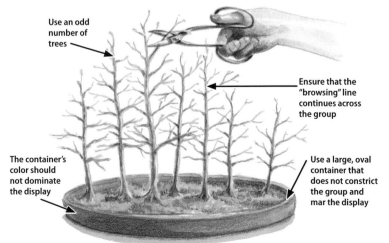

Use an odd number of trees

Ensure that the "browsing" line continues across the group

The container's color should not dominate the display

Use a large, oval container that does not constrict the group and mar the display

**5** Plant the other trees, in the same manner, ensuring that the smallest remaining one is on the right side. Tie the securing wires over the rootballs and spread and firm compost around them. View the group from the "face side" and cut off long and misplaced shoots that spoil the symmetry.

# Creating a Cascade

## ■ Do cascades need a great deal of training?

During its early years, a cascading bonsai requires dedicated attention to ensure that the plant assumes the correct stance and that shoots trail. Initially, the stem is upright, then cascading and trailing. Buy a healthy plant in a pot from a garden center and prune it to shape. When choosing a plant, try to visualize it after it has been pruned. This will ensure that the right plant is bought and that a distinctive display can be created.

## Choosing the Right Plant

Both evergreen and deciduous trees and shrubs can be used to create a cascading style, where plants appear to cascade and trail over the edge of a cliff. It is a picturesque and eye-catching form of bonsai but does need display space in a location with no risk of the plant being knocked and toppled.

Many plants are suitable, other than those which have a definite and natural upright style. The near ground-hugging *Juniperus procumbens*, an evergreen conifer, creates interest throughout the year, while the deciduous, shrub-like *Pyracantha* produces a rich array of flowers, mainly in early summer. Small-leaved Azaleas and Japanese Flowering Cherries, with their evocation of spring, are other flowering shrubs, while the deciduous and often prostrate (it will also grow against walls) *Cotoneaster horizontalis* (Fishbone Cotoneaster) has a natural aptitude as a cascade bonsai.

Small-leaved plants are ideal, as the cascading style is then not smothered and hidden in foliage. *Salix* (Weeping Willows) have a graceful and dainty nature, but they usually grow so fast that frequent pruning is needed, which can spoil their appearance.

*Bonsai with a cascading shape always attract attention. A large pot is usually needed to ensure the cascade remains stable.*

## Cascading Shape Variations

There are several forms of cascading bonsai: some have a main stem that only slightly cascades, while others initially cascade and then trail. Here are three examples:

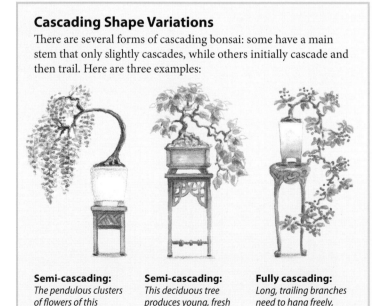

**Semi-cascading:**
The pendulous clusters of flowers of this Wisteria are shown to perfection. They are able to hang freely.

**Semi-cascading:**
This deciduous tree produces young, fresh leaves in spring. In autumn, many also reveal rich colors.

**Fully cascading:**
Long, trailing branches need to hang freely, without any hindrance from the stand. Ensure the pot is stable.

## Breaking the Line

Some cascading bonsai—especially deciduous types—have a branch trained partly across the front of the cascade (on its viewing side) to break the flowing line and to create extra interest in winter.

*Crossing and zigzagging branches create extra visual interest for this cascading bonsai*

# HOW TO CREATE A CASCADING BONSAI

The ground-hugging *Juniperus procumbens*, an evergreen conifer, is ideal as a cascading bonsai. It creates interest throughout the year, but take care that the weight of its branches and foliage do not capsize the pot. Incidentally, pots used for cascades are deeper and heavier than those employed for upright designs.

*Juniperus procumbens* is usually sold in the form *J. p.* 'Nana', which has closely overlapping, awl-shaped, gray-green leaves that form a dense and attractive canopy of foliage. If visually too heavy, pruning away branches and foliage creates a more attractive and appealing shape.

Refining the ends of trailing branches can be left until potting is complete.

Use sharp branch cutters to remove misplaced branches

**1** Select a plant with a trailing nature and transfer to a suitable pot. Use branch cutters to cut away—close to the main stem—branches that are growing in the wrong direction. Stretch out the foliage to enable its shape to be seen, and cut off congested stems.

Hold the plant securely while adding training wires

Ensure that the pot is firm

**2** Use training wires (see pages 34–35) to encourage the main stem to lean. Regularly check that they are not cutting into the bark and remove as soon as the inclination is permanent. A leaning stem encourages branches to cascade in a natural manner. If the trunk has a natural inclination, wiring is not necessary.

Carefully bend the stem into a cascading position

**3** To encourage the plant's main stem to cascade and trail, add further wires so that it is completely trained in this way. After wiring is completed, the branch can be moved into the desired position. Again, regularly check that the bark is not being damaged by wires that are too tight.

If desired, add training wires to side branches

Simplicity is the key to this design

**4** Wiring is not restricted to the trunk. To encourage side branches to create a distinctive shape and not to be congested by their neighbours, also add wires to them. Minimalism is the key to the successful and captivating shape of this style.

Cut off stems that congest the design

It may be necessary to trim the plant's "tail"

**5** After the branches have been wired and manipulated into the desired shape, stand back from the plant. Where stems are congested and spoil the cascading nature, use sharp scissors to cut them away. It is often necessary to cut away some of the plant's "tail" to create an aged appearance.

# Creating a Windswept Bonsai

## ■ How can I produce this style?

It is not difficult to create a windswept style; the key to success is first to select a suitable tree. Buy a tree, growing in a container, from a garden center. When created, the tree should lean dramatically and appear to have been constantly exposed to wind from one direction, and can be imagined to have been growing on an exposed, windy hillside or near the coast. These plants often have a rugged and unkempt appearance, but much dedicated work goes into their training.

## Wind-Plagued Trees

Coastal areas are often plagued by persistent winds, and in such places, Pines can help to create protection from wind. *Pinus pinaster* (Maritime Pine) is native to coastal areas of the western Mediterranean and southern Atlantic coasts of Europe, while *Pinus contorta* (Shore Pine) is native to coastal areas of eastern North America.

*Crataegus* (Hawthorn) has both a North American and European heritage and is well able to survive prolonged coastal wind. *Crataegus coccinea* (Scarlet Haw) and *Crataegus crusgalli* (Cockspur Thorn) are North American, while *Crataegus monogyna* (Common Hawthorn, Quick, or May) is European, including the British Isles.

These Hawthorns are candidates for windswept bonsai, although prostrate evergreen conifers create greater visual impact throughout the year.

## Uniform Direction

When displaying a windswept bonsai, always position them with their stems and foliage blown in the same direction. If mixed, this confuses the eye and does not look quite right. Sometimes this is difficult, as plants may have "face" sides.

← *Windswept bonsai, with their wind-blown nature, immediately capture attention. A clear, unobstructed background ensures the display retains its distinctive nature.*

→ *Trees in wind-exposed coastal areas invariably have more branches on one side than on the other. This also occurs on mountains and moors.*

### Containers for Windswept Bonsai

Containers for this style need to have a rugged appearance, be oval or rectangular, and have a color that pleads severity rather than gentility. Rough-surfaced containers are ideal.

Although containers need to be relatively shallow (unlike those for a cascading style) they must be deep enough to hold sufficient compost to create a firm base for shoots that lean outwards.

### Windswept Shape Variations

In addition to the windswept bonsai featured on the opposite page, there are others, and two that depict a mountainous and wind-exposed area are shown here. They are not as decorative as a windswept tree at the edge of a coastal cliff and have a more rugged nature (see below). Both of them are formed from *Picea jezoensis* (Ezo Spruce, also known as Yezo, Edo, or Yeddo Spruce).

*As well as being shaped and cut to create a windblown nature, bark has been peeled away and the top radically distressed.*

*This wind-blasted design depicts a deadwood stump with part of the bark stripped away to create a weathered appearance.*

# HOW TO CREATE A WINDSWEPT BONSAI

Preferably, select an evergreen conifer with a radically leaning trunk, but if chance does not provide such a plant, it is possible to produce a windswept style from one with a straight stem. The plant is then potted on a slant, and wires (see pages 34–35) are added to ensure the trunk grows in the desired direction.

Evergreen conifers are ideal for this style, as with their year-through foliage they always appear windswept. In nature, the deciduous Hawthorn is famed for surviving wind-blown and exposed places, at the same time producing flowers. It is therefore a candidate for this style.

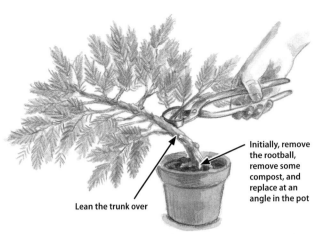

Initially, remove the rootball, remove some compost, and replace at an angle in the pot

Lean the trunk over

**1** Remove the pot and rake compost from the rootball. Temporarily, replace the rootball in its pot and lean the trunk over so that the desired attitude can be assessed. Use branch cutters to cut off all branches growing in the opposite direction to the assumed wind direction.

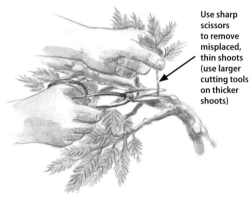

Use sharp scissors to remove misplaced, thin shoots (use larger cutting tools on thicker shoots)

**2** With the plant still leaning over, use sharp scissors to cut out congested branches and small twigs. It is essential that light and air is encouraged to enter the plant, as minimal design is the desired feature. The plant must have a natural, windswept appearance.

Cut branches close to the main stems—do not leave short snags

Remove only 1–2 shoots or branches at a time to ensure too many are not removed

**3** Continue to cut out unwanted branches and small twigs. Cut out upward-growing branches that would spoil the windswept and natural design. Also, cut out clustered shoots that would mar the design and give it a formal outline. Always use sharp tools that make clean cuts.

Occasionally view the plant from about 6' (1.8m) to check the results of pruning

As necessary, cut out further shoots

**4** As well as cutting out upward-growing branches, use sharp cutters to sever those that grow downward. After each pruning, stand back and inspect the plant; there is always a danger of cutting out too many shoots if repeated checks are not made at this stage.

On some plants it is necessary to use training wires

Take care not to damage side shoots

**5** When pruning is completed, wind wires (see pages 34–35) around the trunk to hold it in position. Carefully bend the trunk into the desired direction. Once applied, regularly check the wires to ensure they are not cutting into and damaging the bark.

# Bamboo Bonsai

## ◼ What are the virtues of bamboo bonsai?

Bamboos have many exciting qualities; their stiff, grass-like leaves are uniquely attractive, and they rustle in even the slightest wind, producing relaxing but irregular sounds. Additionally, they are relatively easy to grow (they belong to the grass family and most of those are nature's survivors). Bamboos are excellent for creating size and shape variations in a bonsai collection, producing groves of beautiful stems and leaves.

## Evergreen or Deciduous?

The range of bamboos is wide, and some are evergreen, others semi-evergreen and a few deciduous. However, most bamboos are evergreen, although a few may lose some of their leaves during a very cold winter.

## What Is Bamboo?

Bamboo is an all-embracing term for a group of graceful and elegant plants with cane-like stems that grow from ground level. They are native to tropical, sub-tropical and temperate regions. Bamboos are rampant growers and quick to form clumps. While some bamboos have vigorous and invasive roots—those with a non-invasive, clump-forming nature are best for bonsai. A range of suitable bamboos is given on the opposite page.

   Many bamboos have recently had their names changed, and therefore both new and old names are given here to enable the right plant to be bought.

*Bamboos are mainly hardy, outdoor plants but can be taken indoors, where they create dramatic and eye-catching features, especially when given a setting reminiscent of Asian cultures.*

### Special Care for Bamboo Bonsai

- Drum-shaped containers are ideal for bamboo bonsai, as they create a firm base.
- Every second year, cut dwarf forms back to soil level to keep them small. With large species, when young shoots appear, peel off their sheaths. This reduces the distance between leaf-joints and inhibits growth.
- From spring to the early part of late summer, feed plants every other week with a high-nitrogen fertilizer.
- Keep the compost moist during spring and summer.
- Repot clumps in late spring, every other year.

# Popular Bamboo Bonsai Displays

Three hardy dwarf bamboos suitable for bonsai are *Pleioblastus simonii* (*Arundinaria simonii*), *Pleioblastus pygmaea* (*Arundinaria pygmaea*), and *Pleioblastus auricomus* (*Pleioblastus viridistriatus*). They are all excellent.

Pot up plants in spring, before new shoots appear, and shorten existing canes to compost level. Water the compost, and in early summer, cut off leaves so that smaller ones will develop. Each spring, when new shoots appear, thin out some of the older ones.

Larger bamboos that are also suitable for bonsai include *Fargesia nitida* (*Arundinaria nitida*), *Phyllostachys aurea*, *Phyllostachys nigra*, and *Pleioblastus hindsii* (*Arundinaria hindsii*). They all create dramatic features.

The leaves look especially attractive when the plant is positioned in good light

↗ *The dwarf* Pleioblastus auricomus (Pleioblastus viridistriatus) *has pea-green leaves striped with golden-yellow.*

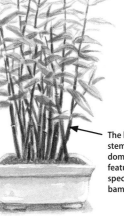

↗ Phyllostachys nigra *has exceptionally beautiful black stems. At first the leaves are mid-green, but they soon darken.*

The black stems are the dominant feature of this spectacular bamboo

## BAMBOO BONSAI INSPIRATIONS

As well as being decorative, one bamboo sometimes grown as bonsai is *Phyllostachys edulis* var. *heterocycla* (*Phyllostachys heterocycla*), which has shoots that can be eaten. Most hardy bamboos develop shoots that are edible, but it is this bamboo that provides the bulk of the bamboo shoots exported from China and Japan. The young shoots, which appear from late spring onwards, are greenish-yellow and spotted with red or brown splashes.

Fargesia nitida (Arundinaria nitida) *is ideal for gardens as well as bonsai.*

*Bamboos look especially dramatic on a patio at night and when their foliage is highlighted by spotlights. Both battery- and mains-powered outdoor spotlights are available. Ensure that mains- powered lights have been installed by a competent electrician.*

# Glossary

**Adult foliage** Produced on mature plants. Some plants have differently shaped and colored adult leaves from those that first appear when a plant is young.

**Apex** The tip of a shoot.

**Bud break** When a leaf-bud opens and reveals a green tip.

**Callus** Corky, hard tissue which forms over a wound; it results in a raised, hard area.

**Cascading** A style of bonsai (see pages 16–17).

**Clasped-to-rock** A style of bonsai (see pages 84–85).

**Compound leaf** A leaf formed of two or more leaflets.

**Conifer** Member of an age-old group of primitive cone-bearing plants. However, some conifers, such as *Taxus baccata* (yew) and *Ginkgo biloba* (maidenhair tree) do not bear cones. Also, some conifers are evergreen, while others are deciduous.

**Cultivar** A plant produced in cultivation and indicating a 'cultivated' variety. Earlier, all variations, whether produced naturally in the wild or in cultivation, were known as 'varieties'. However, as the term 'variety' has been known to gardeners for many decades, it is still frequently used.

**Cut-leaved** Describes a type of leaf that is cut into segments, rather than being entire around its edges.

**Deciduous** A plant that loses its leaves at the beginning of its dormant season. This usually applies to woody plants such as trees, shrubs and some climbers, but it can also apply to some conifers.

**Dieback** This is when the end of a young shoot dies, usually as result of severe weather or fungal infection.

**Evergreen** A plant that continuously sheds and grows new leaves throughout the year and therefore at any one time appears to have complete array of leaves and be 'ever green'.

**Exposed roots** Some bonsai are trained to have roots that are exposed. This creates an impression of maturity and gives the bonsai an attractive quality.

**Face side** Most bonsai have a side that is most attractive and this is known as the face side.

**Formal and upright** A style of bonsai (see pages 16–17).

**Genus** A group of plants with similar botanical characteristics. Within a genus there would be one or more species, each with different characteristics.

**Germination** The process that occurs within a seed when given adequate moisture, air, and warmth. The seed-coat ruptures and the seed-leaf (or leaves) grow up towards the light. At the same time, a root develops. However, to most gardeners germination is when they see the seed-leaves appearing through the surface of compost or soil.

**Groups and landscapes** A style of bonsai (see pages 16–17).

**Habit** The characteristics of a plant.

**Hardy** A plant that in temperate climates is able to be left outside during winter.

**Humidity** The amount of moisture in the atmosphere.

**Indoor bonsai** Where tropical and sub-tropical plants are grown indoors. Sometimes this is known as Chinese bonsai.

**Informal and upright** A style of bonsai (see pages 16–17).

**Internodal** The distance between two leaf-joints (nodes).

**Juvenile leaf** An early leaf which differs markedly from an adult leaf. This an often be seen on some conifers and eucalyptus species.

**Leaning** A style of bonsai (see pages 16–17).

**Loam** A mixture of fertile soil and formed of sand, clay, silt and decomposed organic material.

**Mist-spraying** Using a sprayer to create a fine mist of clean water around plants to increase the humidity.

**Outdoor bonsai** Where trees and shrubs that are hardy in temperate climates are grown outdoors as bonsai. This is sometimes known as Japanese bonsai.

**Peat** Partly decomposed vegetable material, usually acid, that is often used in potting and seed composts. However, cutting this material from peat beds destroys the environment of many birds, animals and insects.

**Perlite** A lightweight material that is added to compost to increase its ability to retain moisture.

**Pinching back** Using fingertips to remove the tips of young shoots. It is a way to increase bushiness and to control the size of a plant.

**Pinching out** See Pinching back.

**Potbound** When a plant fills its container with roots and has no further room for them to grow.

**Repotting** Moving a plant which fills its existing pot with roots into a large one. Alternatively, by cutting away some of the roots a plant can be repotted into a pot of the same size.

**Root-on-rock** A style of bonsai (see pages 84–85).

**Root-over-rock** A style of bonsai (see pages 84–85).

**Root-pruning** Cutting back roots of a potbound plant. With bonsai, this is usually done at the same time as repotting.

**Semi-cascading** A style of bonsai (see pages 16–17).

**Species** A group of plants that breed together and have the same characteristics. Species belong to a genus, which can be formed of one or more species.

**Stone-clasping** A style of bonsai (see pages 84–85).

**Stratification** A method of helping seeds with hard coats to germinate. The seeds are placed between layers of sand and kept cold, usually for the extent of winter.

**Styles of bonsai** There are many different shapes and styles of bonsai, including upright, slanting and cascading (see pages 16–17).

**Succulent** Plants with fleshy, moisture-retentive tissue. Crassulas are an example.

**Synonym** An alternative botanical name for a plant.

**Systemic** An insecticide or fungicide that is able to enter a plant's tissue and give protection against pests and diseases.

**Tender** Describes a plant in a temperate climate that is unable to withstand winter outdoors.

**Twin and multi-trunks** A style of bonsai (see pages 16–17).

**Variety** See Cultivar.

**Windswept** A style of bonsai (see pages 16–17).

**Wiring** A way to shape trunks and branches of a bonsai.

**Wound sealant** A proprietary compound that is used to seal pruning cuts. It prevents the loss of sap.

# Index